PRAISE FOR STAY

"As a longtime meditator, I've seen the power of meditation first hand. *Stay Woke* is a beautiful, action-packed guide to making this vital practice accessible for everyone. Do yourself, your family, and the world a favor and get started now."

MARIE FORLEO
NEW YORK TIMES #1 BESTSELLING AUTHOR OF *EVERYTHING IS FIGUREOUTABLE* AND FOUNDER OF B-SCHOOL

"Imagine going on a journey with a friend who inspires you to become your most resilient, creative, and caring self, no matter the challenges life and the world confront you with. Whether you're facing being marginalized and disempowered or simply want to learn ways to strengthen your mind, our capable guide of *Stay Woke* provides the personally tested and scientifically grounded tools and tips to build a solid way of living during these difficult times. Soak in these words of wisdom from Justin Michael Williams and you may just find yourself smiling more from the inside out, finding more joy, meaning, and connection in your everyday life. What a gift for us all!"

DANIEL J. SIEGEL, MD
NEW YORK TIMES BESTSELLING AUTHOR OF *THE WHOLE BRAIN CHILD*

"Meditation can be wonderfully liberating, or it can be oppressive and frustrating. The difference is that you have to customize meditation to fit your type—your body type, emotion type, mental type, and the flow of your daily life. If we don't invent our own approach to meditation then we'll be oppressed by somebody else's system. *Stay Woke* will teach you how to create a practice that works for you and with you, regardless of what you're dealing with in your life."

LORIN ROCHE AUTHOR OF *THE RADIANCE SUTRAS*

"Justin's is the millennial voice this world has been craving; this book is essential to our collective and individual healing. *Stay Woke* changes the way we look at meditation and taking action, reminding us that the power isn't somewhere out there—it's in each of us."

ELENA BROWER AUTHOR OF *PRACTICE YOU*

"Justin Michael Williams made meditation accessible for me. He demystified it and showed me it didn't have to be such hard work, that I could make it work for me."

DYLLÓN BURNSIDE   ACTOR

"We movement creators, makers, and practitioners often lose ourselves in the need to strategize and react to the everyday ongoing traumas in our society, while neglecting our own mental and physical well-being—fact! Justin Michael Williams's book, *Stay Woke*, debunks the mystery of meditation and gives us the permission that is so needed to create our own personalized practice. He reminds us that by creating space for truth and self-care we are better, more conscious, and more creative allies and leaders."

GINA BELAFONTE   ACTRESS & ACTIVIST

"Justin is an empathetic guide who expertly meets his readers wherever they are on the meditation mountain. Far more than a meditation book, *Stay Woke* is a masterful handbook for life."

CHIP CONLEY   *NEW YORK TIMES* BESTELLING AUTHOR OF *EMOTIONAL EQUATIONS*

"Spirited, empowering, and revolutionary, *Stay Woke* is a guide like none other. Reading this book clears out the clutter, wakes up the mind, and calls us home to our deep soul beauty. Justin Michael Williams is a radical new voice for the times we live in, not afraid to show up fully, go the distance, and embrace the full spectrum of life. Change is here. Rooted and real, authentic and courageous, this guide will change your life and invite you to a whole new realm of possibility. With just the right mix of stories, practices, research, and inspiration, this book shows us how to wield a new kind of magic and calls to action the power to rise up together. P.S.: Thank you Grandmother Baca for your invincible spirit that has moved mountains and reached into all our hearts. The evolutionary power of your spirit now impacts profound change."

SIANNA SHERMAN
FOUNDER AND VISIONARY OF RASA YOGA, RITUAL, AND MYTHIC YOGA FLOW

"*Stay Woke* is for all of us, and especially for those whose life is not always safe and surrounded by privilege. It is for those of us who may worry about paying the rent, or being stopped by the police, or not having a public space that says we belong. *Stay Woke* is a book for those who would not separate spirituality and meditation from a life of being marginalized, or of dealing with trauma. Justin Michael Williams reunites our spiritual life, meditation, with messy, real-life anxiety and struggle. He offers a deep way of being, without requiring we become something we are not. Justin has given us a needed gift that is for all, not just the rich or middle class. Stay Woke."

JOHN A. POWELL
PROFESSOR OF LAW AND OF AFRICAN-AMERICAN & ETHNIC STUDIES AT THE UNIVERSITY OF CALIFORNIA AT BERKELEY; AUTHOR OF *RACING TO JUSTICE*

"*Stay Woke* is an essential guide to conquering the inner landscape of doubt, unraveling it finally so that you may experience freedom and delicious revelation. Justin's instructions are as rhythmic as his music, sure to get you both meditating and dancing to the beat not only of your own drummer, but the drumbeat of your ultimate purpose."

ZHENA MUZYKA   AUTHOR OF *LIFE BY THE CUP* AND FOUNDER OF CLUB MAGIC HOUR

"In *Stay Woke*, Justin Michael Williams provides a blueprint guiding those who have been excluded from holistic self-care practices such as meditation. He offers a relatable set of reflections and tools to help process the existential stress that is rampant in the daily lives of marginalized people. Meditation isn't a practice we engage in to escape the world but a practice we engage in to free us from the emotional and psychological tether that the world weighs upon us. This book is for everyone, especially those who have placed their bodies on the front lines to fight for justice, because that work is only sustainable when we practice self-care."

LATHAM THOMAS
FOUNDER OF MAMA GLOW AND BESTSELLING AUTHOR OF *OWN YOUR GLOW*

STAY
WOKE

S T A Y

justin michael williams

WOKE

a meditation guide
for the rest of us

sounds true

BOULDER, COLORADO

Sounds True
Boulder, CO 80306

This book is not intended as a substitute for the medical recommendations of
physicians, mental health professionals, or other health-care providers. Rather, it is
intended to offer information to help the reader cooperate with physicians, mental
health professionals, and health-care providers in a mutual quest for optimal well-
being. We advise readers to carefully review and understand the ideas presented and
to seek the advice of a qualified professional before attempting to use them.

Published 2020

Book design by Jennifer Miles and Karen Polaski
Illustrations © 2020 Victoria Cassinova

Excerpt from "I Have a Dream" © 1963 Dr. Martin Luther King, Jr.; renewed 1991
Coretta Scott King. Reprinted by arrangement with the Heirs to the Estate of Martin
Luther King, Jr., c/o Writers House as agent for the proprietor, New York, NY.

Printed in South Korea

Library of Congress Cataloging-in-Publication Data
Names: Williams, Justin Michael, author.
Title: Stay woke : a meditation guide for the rest of us / by Justin Michael Williams.
Identifiers: LCCN 2019022807 (print) | LCCN 2019022808 (ebook) | ISBN
    9781683643722 (paperback) | ISBN 9781683644293 (ebook)
Subjects: LCSH: Mindfulness (Psychology) | Meditation. | Social justice. | Conduct of life.
Classification: LCC BF637.M4 W55 2020 (print) | LCC
    BF637.M4 (ebook) | DDC 158.1/2—dc23
LC record available at https://lccn.loc.gov/2019022807
LC ebook record available at https://lccn.loc.gov/2019022808

10 9 8 7 6 5 4 3 2 1

I am you.
You are me.
We are we.
I commit to thee.

This book is dedicated to my people.
We rise together.

contents

The guided practices in *Stay Woke* are available as free audio
downloads at justinmichaelwilliams.com/staywoke.

WE ARE THE

Revolution

PROUD
BLACK +
EDUCATED

We close our eyes,

and we can see a life we haven't started living yet. We see the people we know we were put on this earth to be—and we all know that we were born to do something incredible. We feel it inside. We can see the mother we've always wanted to be, the lover we've always wanted to be, the father, the entrepreneur, the dancer, the artist, the actor, the singer, the leader, and the relationship we've always wanted, the business idea we always think about. But we spend so much time sitting on the sidelines, waiting for the right moment. We sit, and we wait, because when we were younger, somebody told us, "That dream you have is *not* for you." It's not for you because you're too fat, or too old, or too ugly, or too gay, you're not good enough, you're too skinny, too black, or—my favorite—"people like us just don't do that." Whatever. They told us we weren't good enough, and we believed them.

I have a confession to make. This is not really a meditation book.

Yes, I'm going to teach you everything you need to know about meditation, but if you came looking for your typical hippie-type Zen meditation book, you're in the wrong place.

This book is for people who are overwhelmed with obsessive thinking. For people who are dealing with so much anxiety and stress that they have trouble sleeping. For people who have felt ashamed, wounded, not good enough, silenced, or marginalized. For people who feel like there's something missing in their life but can't figure out

IF YOU CAN WORRY, YOU CAN
MEDITATE

what it is. This book will help you pinpoint that wound, heal it, and use it as fuel to live the life you've always dreamed of.

This book is about *taking action*.

This book is about getting rid of that *stuck feeling* that's been gnawing at the back of your mind for all these years.

But, most importantly, this book is for us—*for the people.*

For my black brothers and sisters, this is for you.

For my LGBTQIA+ brothers and sisters, this is for you.

For my women who have had enough, this is for you.

For my starving artists and workaholic creatives, this is for you.

For my conscious entrepreneurs who want to make an impact, this is for you.

For those who have been discrimated against for their otherness, this is for you.

For my social justice warriors, this is for you.

For my tree-loving planet savers, this is for you.

For all people of color and everyone who is woke enough to understand why I'm pointing that out, this is for you.

Throughout my last decade of teaching yoga and meditation, I've been blessed to work with thousands of people, of *all* types of backgrounds, from more than forty countries around the globe, and everyone says the same things: "I've tried meditation, but I can never stick with it," or "I just can't get my mind to slow down," or "I don't believe in meditiation." *And I understand why.*

Meditation—at least the kind of meditation most of us have heard about—
started with a bunch of men who were monks, sitting in the forest. And to
become a monk, you had to release and abandon your entire family, your friends,
all of your internal desires—sex, passion, intimacy—and all of your emotions
and needs, including hunger, thirst, and everything you loved. You had to renounce
all of it, sit under a tree, and devote the rest of your life to spiritual practice
to transcend the suffering of life. Sounds intense, right? It was. So intense that
ancient monks had to use special techniques to help them totally abandon their
worldly desires. The most powerful of these techniques? **Meditation**.

I need to break some news to you. We are not monks. We are modern
people in a high-tech world. We have First World problems and shit to do. We
have iPhones and social media, and we have emotions that keep us connected
to our passions, dreams, and one another. We have relationships, kids, jobs, and
long to-do lists. And if you grew up like me—overcoming systemic oppression,
homophobia, sexism, depression, poverty, toxic masculinity, community
disempowerment, racism, and trauma—you need a different type of meditation.
One that doesn't pretend the struggle doesn't exist.

The reason why so many people try meditation and it doesn't stick is because
they're practicing the wrong kind of meditation, a kind based on renunciation.
This makes meditation feel like doing a chore or even being punished. It can
feel like your mind is going crazy with random thoughts and you have to *force*
yourself to sit still and stop thinking. Sound familiar?

The style of meditation I'm going to teach you in this book is the opposite of
all of that.

And if you're someone who thinks you *can't* meditate because you can't
get your mind to stop thinking, I got some news for ya:

If you can worry, you can meditate.

Worrying and meditation are essentially the same thing, except with worrying, you play out bad scenarios in your head over and over, continuing to return to them throughout your day. Meditation works exactly the same way: the trick is flipping the switch from fear to empowerment. When you worry, you let your thoughts control you; when you meditate, you take your power back.

I'm sure you've heard about some of the benefits of meditation.[1] It:

- Reduces stress
- Helps you sleep better
- Fights off depression
- Relieves anxiety
- Improves your memory
- Improves your focus

- Makes you more productive
- Boosts self-confidence
- Combats prejudice
- Enhances empathy
- Helps with decision-making
- Boosts your immune system

And that's just to name a few. A quick Google search will lead you to a plethora of studies done at major universities around the world highlighting the benefits meditation has on the body, mind, soul, and spirit.

Over the last several years, I've been on a mission to take meditation out of the spiritual echo chamber and bring it to everyday people like you and me. I believe *all* people, of *all* backgrounds, deserve to have access to the truth. So I started asking big questions. How does meditation loosen the grip of our toxic habits, especially when it comes to things like porn, drugs, alcohol, social media, sex, and the incessant need for validation? How does it fit in if we're stressed out, overwhelmed, stretched too thin, and don't have extra time? How does it help us get shit done? How does it impact social justice? Productivity? Relationships? Money? Trauma? Healing? Entrepreneurship? Creativity? How does it help us overcome the obstacles that hold us back from our inherent greatness? The answers to those questions gave birth to the style of meditation that I'm going to teach you in this book.

I'd like to introduce you to **Freedom Meditation**, a practice that connects us with the most powerful version of our own selves— the Self that's deep down inside, untouched and unscathed by all the bullshit we've gathered over the years—and sets it free.

LET'S GIVE IT A TEST RUN. Place both hands over your heart and take three slow, deep breaths—5 counts in and 5 counts out. Feel your chest rise and fall with each breath. Make sure you don't breathe too fast. Really slow it down—5 long counts in, 5 long counts out. Notice how your entire body expands a little bit with each inhale and contracts and gets smaller with each exhale. After at least three breaths, keep a hand over your heart and answer these questions: What's the *real* dream for your life? And why are you still holding yourself back from getting there? **What's the *real* reason?**

And don't tell me, "I don't know." If you're reading this book, I know you're ready to take *some* part of your life to the next level—so what is it? What's really holding you back? Drop in and think about it for a sec. I promise we'll have an opportunity to work through this together as you learn to meditate. If you're having trouble identifying what's stopping you, don't worry—we'll be unpacking this more a little later in the book. In all cases, it's better to think about this now than to wait until life hits you upside the head with a dramatic situation to wake you up, like it did to me.

I've got a little story for you. In 2012, my grandmother, whom I was very close to, was diagnosed with stage 4 cancer, and the doctors told her she only had a few months to live. This rocked my world like nothing I had ever experienced before. You have to understand, my Baca, as I called her, was my best friend. She was my light, my coach, my everything. Anyone who is superclose to their grandmother knows what I mean. It's a special relationship unlike anything else in the universe.

I was devastated when I got the news, so I flew to my hometown, Pittsburg, California, to be with her. The moment I arrived, she kicked everyone else out of the room, sat me down, looked me in the eyes, and asked me a question that literally changed the trajectory of my entire life.

She asked, "If you were in my shoes and knew you were going to die in two months, what would you do?"

I started trembling. I felt the tears well up, but a childhood of being told, "Only faggots cry" blockaded my tears like a dam holds back a stream. Before I could even think, the answer erupted out of my mouth with a roar of emotion from the deepest part of my soul: "I would stop everything that I'm doing and record an album."

My Baca smiled, because she was a believer all along. I, on the other hand, was frozen in some combination of shock, joy, and longing, like what I imagine the disciples felt when they saw Jesus ascend from the tomb. The ghost of my truth had been resurrected.

Here's the thing. I had always wanted to make music. It had been my dream ever since I was a little boy, but I never thought I was good enough—I had let all the kids at school who teased me about being gay make me feel like I sucked at everything. They said I was "too feminine" when I sang or performed, and being feminine when you're a little black boy growing up in the hood means getting beat up. Plus, when I looked around at the people closest to me, there were very few signs of anyone making money doing something they loved. The idea of working and *enjoying* your work, or being passionate about your work, was almost nonexistent in our community, where people were barely making ends meet.

The paradox of my childhood was love and abuse, protection and violence, acceptance and "Don't talk about it." My family sacrificed a lot and did the best they could to provide an abundant life for five kids and shield us from the danger of our environment, but still there was a lot of trauma. There were gunshot holes on the exterior of our house. And one of my most vivid memories is calling 911 trying to protect my mom from my violent stepfather, who choked and beat and abused her until we finally escaped to live with my grandparents.

All I wanted was to make a lot of money and be successful enough to *get out*. And I'm so grateful to say that I did. I got a full-ride academic scholarship to the University of California, Los Angeles (UCLA), started my own marketing company at twenty years of age, and was making six figures by the time I was twenty-six. I had celebrity clients, a black BMW, and an apartment two blocks from the beach in Los Angeles. Most people would say I was "living the dream."

But it was the wrong dream. It was a dream based on a desire to *leave*, not a desire to *fly*. To fulfill cultural expectations based on oppressive traditions;

to do whatever I could to be loved, validated, and accepted by my mom and dad; to be "successful" as defined by everyone else's expectations; to save and rescue everybody, because I was the smart one, the successful one, the one who "made it," numbing my *real* dream in the process of overfunctioning and overachieving. Is any of this sounding familiar?

You see, those of us who grow up in the struggle—whatever particular struggle that may be—are not given an opportunity to dream big enough. When you grow up with violence and abuse, you dream of safety. When you grow up living from paycheck to paycheck, you dream of security. When you grow up in a broken home, you dream of stability. When you grow up being teased for being different, your dream is to belong. When you grow up marginalized, you dream of the same basic rights that seem to be afforded to everyone else by default. So of course you forget to dream bigger. Of course the dream you had when you were a kid gets pushed to the recesses of your mind. It hurts too much to hold on to that dream—the dream you had before you knew about the struggle. Before you knew about racism. Before you knew about slavery. Before you knew about suffrage. Before you knew about the Holocaust. Before you knew about divorce. Before you knew about depression. Before you knew about drugs. Before you knew about domestic violence. Before you knew about systemic oppression.

Underneath all that bullshit, there's a dream. It might be dormant and covered in complacency, but it's still there. It hasn't abandoned you. Meditation will help you wake it up. And if there's a new dream knocking on your door, meditation will help you answer it.

I remember the first day I met with my meditation teacher Lorin Roche like it was yesterday. We met up at the end of Ocean Park Boulevard in Santa Monica, California, on a warm April morning at 9:45 a.m. The beach was mostly empty, since it was a weekday. The sun was shining and the waves were crashing just a few feet away as we sat together with our feet buried in the sand. I was skeptical and jaded from several failed attempts at meditation, but I had heard Lorin was the real deal, so I allowed myself to be open to the experience. I didn't know it then, but that one meetup would shift the course of my life forever. Lorin become my mentor. He took a tender, young, and broken Justin under his wing and taught me everything he knew. I developed Freedom Meditation directly from what I learned from him.

I used to be riddled with anxiety and sadness. I used to constantly compare myself to other people. I felt like I didn't belong. I craved external validation. I would lie awake in bed at night obsessing over work, money, and relationships. It was like I had a void that could never be filled. But the meditation practice I learned from Lorin healed all that. It helped me release my unhealthy relationships with caffeine, drugs, alcohol, and meaningless sex, and it gave me access to a wellspring of power and radiance that existed underneath the haze of all my vices. Meditation empowered me with intuitive guidance, fast decision-making, and a clear state of mind so that I could break through my toxic patterns, find my purpose, and live the life that had been waiting for me all along. I promise to teach you everything I know in this book.

I met Lorin nine months after my Baca passed away. Within three years, my life completely changed. My debut album, *Metamorphosis*, premiered in the iTunes top 20 pop charts alongside Taylor Swift and Britney Spears. Since then I have performed on stages alongside Deepak Chopra and Chaka Khan, and my music has been downloaded millions of times in more than sixty countries around the globe. I travel the world speaking, teaching, and performing and make more money now than I did before I took that big leap into the unknown of the music industry.

But this isn't about me. This is about you, your journey, your life, and you moving toward *your* full potential.

Part 1 of *Stay Woke* has one goal: to teach you how to meditate in a way that is customized to fit in with your messy modern life. You'll learn how to stop self-sabotage, overcome fear and self-doubt, and enhance your intuition so you can finally make sense of all that random thinking. I'll also teach you how to discover your *unique energy signature*—the special sauce that turns meditation into an unbreakable habit. Once you complete this ten-step recipe, you will have created a personalized Daily Meditation Ritual that *you can do on your own, for life*.

Part 2 of the book is formated buffet style—thirty-three grab-and-go minipractices designed to help you with anxiety, stress, sleep, focus, productivity, purpose, intuition, self-love, and social justice. After you've completed all the steps in part 1 and cooked up your own meditation practice, you can flip open to any page of part 2 and enjoy the minipractices at your own pace or work through them with the Daily Practice Plan on page 294.

Meditation will give you the opportunity to go inside, and feel, and know, and touch, and take responsibility for your gifts and talents so that you can finally stop wasting time, move beyond your fears, and wake up to the life you were born to live. And not just for yourself—for your family, for your community, for the planet, and *for the people*.

I'll warn you, though: it ain't easy being woke.

Saying that you're "woke" isn't just about knowledge. And it isn't just some catchy hashtag that randomly popped up on your news feed or favorite blog. The word *woke* came from my ancestors. It was created by black people in the 1960s who had to fight for their existence. By people who had to stare segregation and oppression in the face yet still keep hope for a brighter future. And even though the word has been misused and misappropriated by journalists around the world without apology, we—the people—cannot abandon woke. We *need* woke. "Woke" isn't just some throwaway word, like "fleek" or "bae." It's sacred. If you are black, or Native, or trans, or poor, or disabled, or a woman, or anyone who's had to face an uphill battle just to enjoy the freedom that is your birthright, you *better* Stay Woke. Many of our ancestors didn't have the luxury to think about things like meditation, mental health, manifesting, and life purpose; they had to sacrifice their passions to create stability and the possibility of change for the future generation. We are that generation. We have been paid for. And we cannot take that for granted.

Staying woke isn't just about awareness. It is a call to action. And it matters most when you feel like giving up.

STAY WOKE

STAY WOKE you are worthy. STAY WOKE you are ready. STAY WOKE you can do this. STAY WOKE you are not alone. STAY WOKE you are not broken. STAY WOKE you have the power within you. STAY WOKE don't give up. STAY WOKE it's okay to cry. STAY WOKE I know the road has been tough. STAY WOKE there are better days ahead.

STAY WOKE. STAY WOKE. STAY WOKE.

I have tears in my eyes as I write this. I cry for the losses in our communities. We have gone through so much. More than most people could ever imagine. So please, my brothers and sisters, STAY WOKE. Don't go to sleep. We need you.

I call to you. I pray to you. I scream to you so loud that you remember who you really are. I remind you of your greatness. I remind you of where you came from.

I REMIND YOU THAT YOU ARE ROYALTY.

We have been passed the torch. Yes, there's much more work to do, but the only way we can rise up is if we stand together and say YES to our lives, YES to our dreams, and YES to the greatness that lives inside of each of us.

STAY WOKE your community needs you.

STAY WOKE your family needs you to change.

STAY WOKE the future generations are counting on you.

STAY WOKE to the ways in which you internalize shame.

STAY WOKE in times of trial. STAY WOKE in times of pain. STAY WOKE I know it'll get better. STAY WOKE I know there will be brighter days.
STAY WOKE we need you to make it. STAY WOKE I'll be by your side.
STAY WOKE we'll get there together. STAY WOKE and we'll never die.
STAY WOKE even when you're alone. STAY WOKE I'll hold your hand.
STAY WOKE we can lean on each other. STAY WOKE I'll be a better man.
STAY WOKE please know that I love you. STAY WOKE please know that I care.
STAY WOKE I'm always beside you. STAY WOKE even when you think I'm not there. STAY WOKE my beautiful people. STAY WOKE beautiful people that shine.

I care about you so much. I just want you to thrive.

STAY WOKE—the revolution starts inside.

Thank you for allowing me to be your guide. It is an honor I do not take for granted. We are on a great journey together. And it all starts . . . now.

part 1

meditation for THE PEOPLE:

a recipe for freedom

Most families of color don't have 400-year-old jewels or priceless artwork to pass down from our ancestors, so recipes are kept close to the hearts of our grandmothers and passed down like sacred family heirlooms. My Baca started teaching me to cook when I was about fifteen. Every holiday, all the boys would be watching football while I would stay in the kitchen learning every secret to her mouthwatering recipes. Learning to cook from my Baca was all about intuition; she kept recipes in barely legible scribbles on the backs of old envelopes, and the most accurate metric used was "a pinch of this" and "a dash of that." My Baca's recipes were always made to taste, not to numbers. So learning from her required the full presence of all of my senses.

Whether it was collard greens, dressing, fried chicken, or gravy, I knew that my Baca's favorite trick was to add a little bit of sugar (or, as she would call it, "shuga") to everything—because life is always better with a little sweetness. I'm going to teach you how to build your Daily Meditation Ritual the same way my Baca taught me how to cook: with loose guidelines, room for experimentation, and, of course, a pinch of shuga.

As we get started, I want you to remember this one important rule: *This is your recipe—and it's always okay to make substitutions.*

I've made many substitutions to my Baca's recipes over the years to accommodate my ever-evolving dietary restrictions. Some have come out great, and others have been terrible. If your substitutions don't work, you can always come back to the original recipe. Let's get cooking.

CHAPTER

1

the truth will set us free

THE IDEA THAT YOU HAVE TO GET YOUR MIND TO STOP THINKING IN ORDER TO

The reason most people suck at meditating is the same reason most people suck at cooking: they have the wrong recipe. Neither cooking nor meditation is hard, but most of us have picked up bad habits, myths, and misunderstandings that keep us from being successful in the kitchen or in our practice. My Baca would always say, "The truth will set you free." The same thing applies here.

The following five myths, as I like to call them, are the main roadblocks that cause people to give up their meditation practice prematurely or never get started altogether. I know you're probably ready to learn to meditate by now, but if we don't cover these five myths first, your meditation practice **will not last**, so please read them carefully. Once you get a handle on these myths, you'll be primed and prepped to jump into your personal meditation workshop with me and a few special guests.

MYTH 1 I CAN'T CONCENTRATE LONG ENOUGH.

When we are introduced to meditation, most of us are told that it's about focus and concentration . . . especially if you concentrate on your breath, a candle flame, a flower, or something "spiritual." A lot of us say, "I have trouble focusing." But the real reason why we have such a hard time concentrating during meditation is because we're trying to focus on something boring. I need you to know this: the reason why most meditation apps and techniques don't stick is often because

MEDITATE **IS A LIE!**

they force you to concentrate on things that you don't really care about. And if you're like me, concentrating on my heartbeat, a flower, a flame, or on my breath might be cute for a day or two, but it doesn't work over the long term.

Throughout this book, you will learn to customize meditation around *something you love* so focusing can be natural and easy. Meditation should feel like a vacation you give to yourself every day. It's the ultimate act of self-care.

I will *never* ask you to focus on something boring. I promise.

MYTH 2 I CAN'T GET MY MIND TO STOP THINKING.

In every single workshop I teach, people say things like this:

"I just can't meditate."
"My mind is always going crazy."
"As soon as I sit down to meditate, it's like my thoughts beat me to the punch."

READ THIS CAREFULLY: The idea that you have to get your mind to stop thinking in order to meditate *is a lie*!

Asking the mind to stop thinking is like asking your heart to stop beating, and we know how silly that would be. Not to mention that trying to get the mind to stop thinking is just another form of thought! The mind is intelligence. It's how we download intuitive messages. It's how we manifest our dreams and goals. It's how we relate to people. So instead of trying to get the mind to stop thinking, we want to learn to get the mind to work *for us* rather than against us.

You must learn to anchor your thoughts—to use your thoughts in service of your growth—instead of letting them spin you out of control. I'll teach you exactly how to do that in this book.

MEDITATION IS NOT ABOUT RELAXING; MEDITATION IS ABOUT BECOMING MORE ALIVE.

MYTH 3   I HAVE A HARD TIME RELAXING WHEN I SIT STILL.

I'll warn you now: sometimes your meditations might not feel all that relaxing. You might feel anxious, nervous, excited, agitated, sad, et cetera. This doesn't mean your meditations are always going to feel intense and dark, but they definitely won't always feel peaceful.

When you first sit down to meditate, everything you've been pushing down is going to come up to the surface. Allow it. Including the bad shit and crazy thoughts. Those of us who have grown up with some level of trauma have gotten very skilled at pushing things down, especially when it's painful or dark. But we all know what happens when you push things down for too long: the pressure explodes in some part of your life where it doesn't belong. Meditation is a safe place for all of your emotions to arise without wreaking havoc on your life.

The way to enjoy your practice is to release all expectations of what you think it's *supposed to be*. Your life changes every day, and your meditations will too. Welcome it.

Meditation is not about relaxing; meditation is about *becoming more alive*.

MYTH 4   I HEARD MEDITATION IS AGAINST MY RELIGION.

Although my spiritual beliefs have evolved since I was a kid, I grew up strictly Christian and Catholic. So when I started doing meditation and yoga, my family was totally freaked out. So freaked out that my mom and Baca tried to have an intervention, because they thought I had joined a cult. They said we needed to have a "serious talk" about the crystals, and the prayer beads, and the new words I was using, like "the universe" and "namaste." By their reaction, you would've thought I had told them I was selling my soul; little did they know, I was doing the exact opposite. I explained to them that meditation is not a religion. It doesn't require you to pray to any mysterious deities, believe in any secondary gods, chant in a foreign language, or call on any spirits. Meditation does not interfere with or conflict with any spiritual or religious practices at all.

If you're a spiritual person, think of meditation as a supplement to your spiritual practices—something to enhance and strengthen your connection to your source of Higher Power.

Prayer is when you're speaking to your source of Higher Power, and meditation is when you're listening to the messages coming back to you.

Sometimes throughout this book, I'll use words like "God" or "the universe." If that makes you have a gut reaction, like it did to my family, always feel free to replace those words with whatever Higher Power you believe in. All beliefs are welcome here.

PRAYER IS WHEN YOU'RE SPEAKING TO YOUR SOURCE OF HIGHER POWER AND MEDITATION IS WHEN YOU'RE LISTENING TO THE MESSAGES COMING BACK TO YOU.

MYTH 5 I KINDA FEEL LIKE I MEDITATE WHEN I [INSERT PHYSICAL ACTIVITY HERE].

People always tell me things like this:

"Running is my meditation."
"Singing is my meditation."
"Working out is my meditation."

And while you *can* get into a mindful or meditative state while engaging in those activities, they are not meditation.

There is a difference between practicing mindfulness and practicing meditation.

Practicing mindfulness is the art of practicing awareness, acceptance, and nonjudgment while engaging in any activity. Sometimes that activity *is meditation*, but you can practice mindfulness while doing anything. For example, frying chicken mindfully might include sending lovingkindness to the chicken for giving up its life for your sustenance, consciously smelling the scent of each spice as you add it to your seasoning, and carefully removing the chicken from the pan just before it reaches the perfect hue of golden brown. Being mindful is a practice of presence while *doing something*.

Practicing meditation is a little different. Meditation encourages us to release all that external stimuli and turn our awareness inward. It's less about *doing* and more about *being*.

Most of us are trying so hard to avoid being alone with ourselves. But if we cannot be alone with ourselves, how can we ever expect to know who we really are? Freedom Meditation combines the best of mindfulness and meditation into one practice to help you cultivate an intimate relationship with your Highest Self.

I want you to fall in love with you. Just you—alone.

The real transformation begins when you drop all the distractions and *allow meditation to be your meditation*.

WELCOME TO YOUR PERSONAL MEDITATION WORKSHOP

Now that you've learned the truth about meditation, I'd like to welcome you to your personal meditation workshop. I've structured the rest of part 1 so you can go through it like an interactive workshop with me—kind of like a cooking class. I'd like you to meet a few special people who I've invited to take this class with you. Say hello to . . .

AMBER   A recently married, busy young mom who has overcome many struggles to create stability in her life. She does everything she can to provide a happy, stable home for her family but is struggling to find time to take care of herself. When she gets too stressed or tired, she ends up yelling at her daughter or snapping at her partner, which puts her in a spiral of shame and guilt. Amber grew up Christian and continues to raise her family with a strong belief in God, but sometimes she feels conflicted between her religious beliefs and her alternative curiosity about the universe, spirituality, and the power of the mind. Amber's tried a couple of twenty-one-day meditation challenges and loved them, but she always reverts back to her normal stressed-out state as soon as the twenty-one days are up, so she's not sure if investing more time into meditation is worthwhile—especially since she has so much else on her plate. Plus every time she tries to meditate, her mind goes wild. She just can't stop thinking. Amber is in desperate need of some self-love and self-care, and she hopes Freedom Meditation will help . . . fast.

LISA   On the outside, Lisa looks like the average, happy-go-lucky American woman, but internally she is experiencing a revolution. She's been exploring different workshops, events, and online courses to bring some excitement and passion into her life, and all of the new information she's been learning is waking her up to the grave injustices in the world—she never realized she was so privileged. Lisa has a deep love of nature and the environment, and she desperately wants to use her privilege to impact marginalized communities, but she is struggling to find her voice in the woke movement. Lisa grew up in what most people thought was the perfect home, but, as she recently posted on social media, she's a sexual assualt survivor and has been struggling internally for a while now. When she closes her eyes, a lot of painful emotions and memories come up, and she doesn't know what to do with them. She feels bad complaining, considering she's had it pretty easy compared to most people, and she hopes meditation will help heal her trauma so she can ignite that spark that's been missing from her life. Lisa's done a bit of meditation in her yoga classes over the years, and she even tries to practice at home sometimes, but she can't seem to find the discipline to keep going consistently. Every time she meditates, her mind gets relaxed for a few minutes at best, but then she tries to hold on to that state, and it disappears. Sitting still is also hard for Lisa, so she prefers power yoga, exercise, or some sort of movement to calm her mind when she's overwhelmed. Lisa heard Freedom Meditation is perfect for people like her, so she's looking forward to giving it a shot.

DAVID   A young and talented Latino actor-artist-creative who's been trying to break into the entertainment industry, David is struggling because he has too many ideas and not enough money. David's plan is to eventually make enough cash to fund one of his many creative projects so that he can leave his side hustle and become a full-time artist, but it's taking a lot longer than he expected. Sometimes he feels like he's making progress, but life always seems to throw him a curveball that knocks him off base and into a mild depression. When he gets depressed, he drinks a lot, smokes too much weed, and gets stuck scrolling through hookup apps in search of validation. He's conscious enough to know those habits aren't healthy for him, but sometimes he just needs the escape. Everyone keeps telling David to try meditation, and he's done it a couple of times before, but if he's really honest, he thinks it's boring AF. All of his creative friends talk about how amazing meditation is, but he just doesn't get all the hype. Maybe he's doing it all wrong? He can't sit still. And his mind stays busy—thinking about his to-do list, money, food, and sex—and then he gets mad at himself for thinking about those things. David feels like there's a glass ceiling above him that he just can't break through, and he is starting to realize that maybe he's sabotaging himself. He wants to go to therapy to explore some of this, but he can't afford it, so he's taking one last shot with meditation in hopes that it will give him the breakthrough he needs.

JORDAN   Smart, educated, and good at a lot of things, Jordan has no idea what he wants to do with his life. He is feeling a little lost; nothing really stands out as the one single *purpose* for his life. Everyone is telling him to "relax" and "take his time," but deep down he feels embarrassed and nervous that his friends and family will look at him as a failure if he doesn't figure it out soon. He's debating between finding a job close to home (even though he doesn't really want to), traveling abroad, or going back to school—he changes his mind daily. Jordan's been feeling pretty bored and lethargic lately, and he has been wasting a lot of time, which makes him feel even worse. His best friend keeps telling him to try meditation, but he's skeptical about it—he's a bit analytical and doesn't believe in all the "woo-woo" spiritual things. Plus, when he looked up online videos of people meditating, he saw them doing all these weird chants and prayers, and he just isn't into all that stuff. But even though Jordan's not sure if meditation is right for him, he's open to giving it a try because it's had such a positive impact on his best friend. He just hopes he can find the motivation to stick with it once he learns, because he's definitely ready for a big change and wants to find the clarity to move on to the next chapter of his life with confidence.

And then there's me, Justin, your guide and teacher, who's constantly in the deep process of self-actualization and discovery. I'm a self-help junkie, and my biggest goal in life is to fulfill my calling and mission on this planet . . . but that desire has a shadow, too. It has often led me down the rabbit hole of perfectionism and has caused me to become your classic type-A workaholic who selfishly pushes everything and everyone else aside in the *pursuit of purpose*. I'm a creative at heart, but I've always had a business mind and sometimes struggle to reconcile my desire to be successful with my desire to be artistically free. I am the child of an African American father and a Persian mother, but my mom was adopted into an Italian family. As you can imagine, I grew up with quite the identity crisis. I was too whitewashed for the black kids, too black for the white kids, too feminine for the straight kids, and too closeted for the gay kids—so I decided to become a smart kid. My biggest wounds are the feeling of not being enough and the fear of rejection, which caused me to hold myself back for much of my early life, but meditation changed everything for me.

And, of course, there's you. The one reading this book, with your own particular questions, struggles, dreams, and desires. All of the answers, big and small, are waiting for you inside of this practice. Freedom Meditation has changed my life and the lives of thousands of my students around the globe. Now it's your turn.

We are going on a great journey together. Here are some final tips to make sure you get the most out of your experience:

- **Go in order.** Be sure to read each of the next ten chapters in order. Each one builds upon the information in the chapter prior. After you're done, you won't need to go through each of the individual steps anymore— meditation will become easy and effortless.

- **Do the guided practices.** Learning to meditate is like learning to swim. You can read about swimming as much as you want, but you will never actually learn until you jump in the pool. Be sure to pause and test out all of the guided practices. You can either read them or download the guided audio versions at justinmichaelwilliams.com/staywoke (they're free to download for everyone—my gift to you).

- **Go at your own pace.** This book is designed so that you can read at a speed that fits with your life. If you read one chapter per day, you will have created your Daily Meditation Ritual in ten days. But you can also just read it on the weekends or binge and do it all at once. It's up to you. This is deep and transformative work, so if you get overwhelmed, pause. **It's important that you do not allow meditation to become another stressor in your life.** Do what feels right for you.

- **Make sure your phone is on silent.** Your phone will distract you from getting in tune with the most important person in this workshop: you. Every time you read, get in the practice of turning your phone on silent or airplane mode. If you use your phone to set a timer for the practices or to listen to the audio, make sure it doesn't ring or vibrate at all. This is important.

- **Check out the science.** You'll notice citations scattered throughout the book, many of which come from the Greater Good Science Center at the University of California, Berkeley, a research institute dedicated to investigating social and emotional wellbeing. Meditation isn't just some spiritual magic trick. Much of what I'm teaching you has been scientifically and quantitatively proven. If you're skeptical (or just like to geek out on the research, like I do), there are plenty of goodies for you in the back of the book.

- **Join the community.** No major movement of radical change was ever accomplished by a single person alone, so why would we expect to create radical change in our lives all by ourselves, with no help or support? The system that keeps us separate is the system that keeps us broken, so please take a moment to go to justinmichaelwilliams.com/staywoke to join the free online platform I've created just for you so that you don't have to do this all by yourself. You'll find tons of guided meditations, videos, and resources there to help you on your journey.

- **Finding understanding.** There will be moments in this book when I say something that you think doesn't apply to you. I may speak specifically to black people, gay people, women, or another marginalized group. When that happens, don't skim over the pages. Use it as a chance to practice understanding the struggle of someone who is unlike you. The road to understanding is the road to equality.

- **Experience everything.** You may feel emotions or have realizations that are new and scary to you. Give yourself the FREEDOM to welcome it all. That's how breakthroughs happen. There are no rules. Everything you are feeling is valid.

I know you're busy, so I promise to always keep the practices concise, powerful, and packed with guidance that you can apply to your life right away.

With a little commitment, meditation can be the biggest gift of healing, and I am honored to share these teachings with you in hopes that you will unlock every door that your heart has been knocking on, break down every barrier that has stood in your way, and open up to the life that you deserve to live.

You will be tested, challenged, and tempted by distraction as you continue to read this book. When your commitment is being tested, remember to refocus your priorities and attention onto *your* calling. Stay the course, and your life will totally transform. The practice I'm going to teach you has helped thousands of people from all over the world find fulfillment. Follow it step by step, and you will find your unique path as well.

If you are ready to say **YES** to your dreams, your purpose, and your mission on this planet, take out a pen and sign your signature on the line below. This is an energetic agreement between you and the universe to affirm that you are committed to the journey.

And if there's any more info you need, reach out to me and my team. We are here for you.

WE RISE TOGETHER.

I AM COMMITTED
[sign here]

Essential Points from This Chapter

- Meditation is not about forcing yourself to focus and concentrate. If you build a practice around *something you love*, meditation becomes natural and easy.

- Don't try to get your mind to stop thinking—you can't! In Freedom Meditation, you'll learn to get your thoughts to work *for you* rather than letting them spin you out of control.

- Meditation doesn't always feel relaxing—and it's not supposed to. Freedom Meditation enhances your connection to all thoughts, feelings, sensations, and emotions to help you become more *alive*.

- Meditation is not a religion and does not conflict with any spiritual or religious practices.

- While biking, swimming, singing, dancing, or engaging in another activity that puts you in a state of flow might feel meditative, those things are *not* meditation. Meditation invites us to release external stimuli and turn our awareness inward. It's less about *doing* and more about *being*.

- Your workshop buddies are:
  Amber, the busy mama
  David, the creator
  Lisa, the survivor
  Jordan, the skeptic on the search for purpose

CHAPTER

2

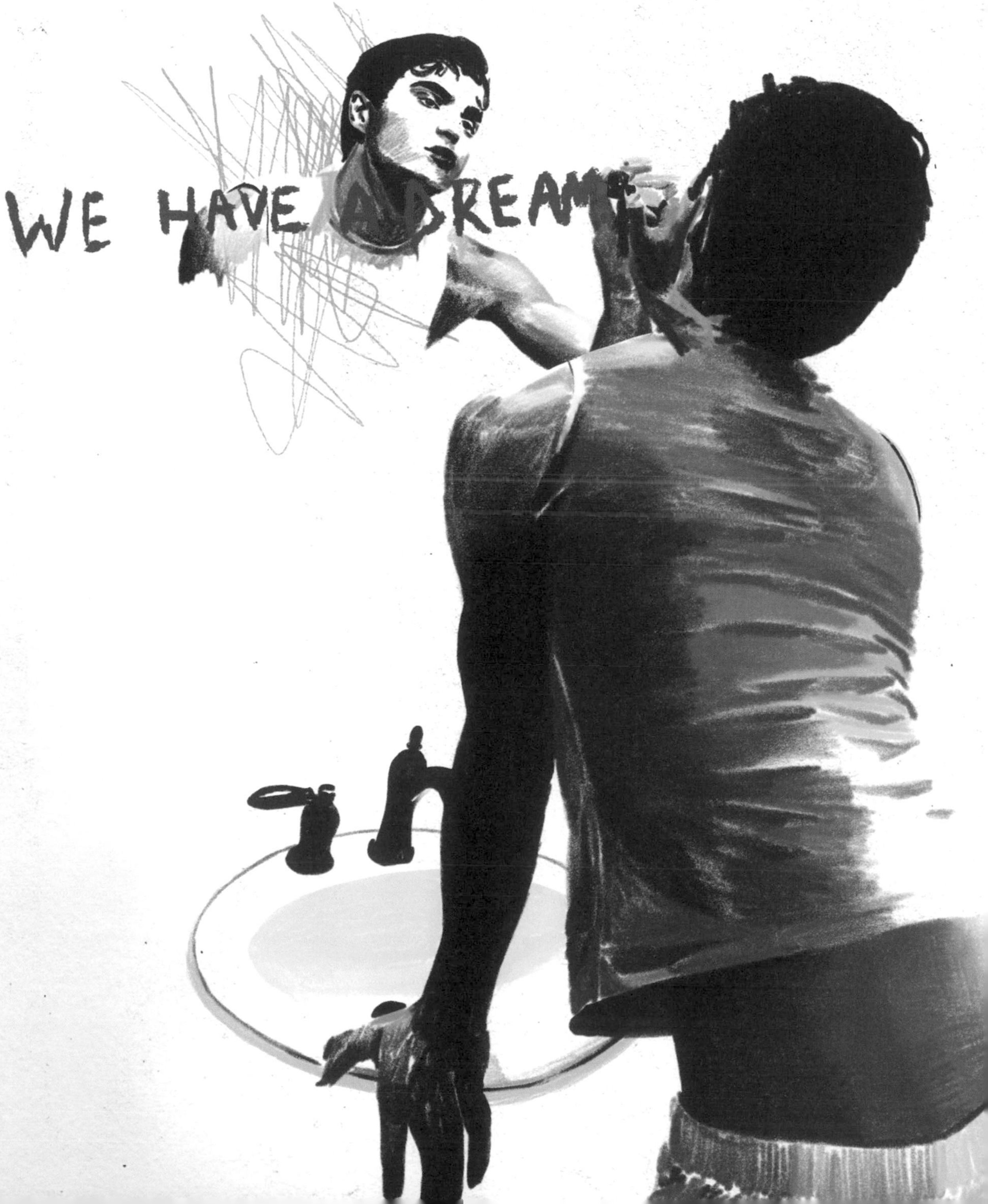
WE HAVE A DREAM

Freedom Meditation helps you reach your dreams and goals faster, but if you don't know your dreams and goals, meditation can't help you get there. It's time to dissect the vision for your life and weed out anything that's based on outdated traditions, self-doubt, other people's expectations, or a need for validation. Getting clear on your dreams is the first ingredient in the recipe for Freedom Meditation. Before you start to refine your vision, however, I want you to hear something important: **Your thoughts don't create your reality. I REPEAT: Your thoughts do not create your reality.**

Don't worry—I'm not debunking every self-help book you've ever read or saying that every life coach or guru is lying. But taken out of context, the idea that your thoughts create your reality is harmful. The true reality is, some of your trauma was never your fault to begin with, and overcoming it is not just a matter of thinking your way through it.

Your thoughts *don't* create your reality when you live in the South Bronx and suffer from the highest levels of asthma in the United States, affecting your health and wellbeing for the rest of your life, or when you live in Flint, Michigan, and your brain is damaged by poisoned water that your country won't do anything about. Your thoughts *don't* create your reality when you're a little girl who is molested by her stepfather before the age of six. Your thoughts *don't* create your reality when you're a young black boy who gets shot walking down the street just because you're wearing a hoodie. Thoughts didn't create the reality of the victims of 9/11, refugees seeking asylum, children slain in school shootings, black trans women who are disproportionately impacted by hate crimes and fatal violence, Native people whose lands have been stolen, or the millions of people around the world overcoming sexism, racism, oppression, genocide, environmental ruin, homophobia, xenophobia, stress inequity, or [insert the injustice of your choice here].

Your thoughts influence your reality, but they don't create it. Reality is cocreated among all of us, in both thoughts and actions.

Actions affect people.

Actions create change.

Actions break patterns.

Thoughts are only part of the equation.

This is why we meditate. So that we can get up off of our asses and take action. Meaningful action. For ourselves, our families, our communities, and the environment.

We are not separate. We are not in a bubble. We are not in our own silos. We are all affecting one another. All of us, together, are creating the quantum interwoven fabric that we live in.

So don't let yourself be bullied by this supposed "law of attraction," which, like many laws, was written by white folks with top-shelf privilege and is well overdue for a more inclusive amendment.

WHAT NOBODY TELLS YOU ABOUT "SETTING INTENTIONS"

Most thought leaders of the modern age preach about the power of vision and intention, but very few explain how it all works beyond the esoteric "laws of the universe." I'm as spiritual and New Agey as you can get, but there's nothing I love more than learning a little neuroscience that proves what the mystics have known for all these years.

Let's get sciencey for a second.

I'd like to introduce you to an important function of your brain called the *reticular activating system*, also known as the RAS. I first learned about the power of the RAS from my dear friend Eva Clay, clinical sexologist, psychotherapist, and neuroscience nerd. The RAS is the part of the brain that helps you notice things. For example, when you are running out of the house and realize you don't have your car keys, your RAS blurs everything out to help you home in and find the keys. Or when you're rummaging through your purse to find your ChapStick, your RAS tunes your hand to feel for the exact shape and size of that ChapStick—you'll know right away whether or not you're holding ChapStick or grabbing a similarly sized lip gloss or mascara. The RAS helps your brain zero in on exactly what it's looking for all the time.[1]

Science has proven the amount of storage we have in our brains is limited. We can only process so much at one time. But every day billions of stimuli fly at us both internally and externally, fighting for our attention. Since the brain cannot process all of those stimuli together, it uses the RAS to decide what is important and what is not. Every image you see, color you process, conversation you hear, emotion you feel, and thought you have is filtered through your RAS. Everything that is deemed useless gets filtered out, ignored, and discarded, while everything that is considered necessary for your survival gets processed and stored. Even as you read this book, there will be information your brain determines is not important or relevant to your growth, so you won't remember it. But you will also find concepts that are immediately relevant to your life *right now*, so your RAS will lock them in.

Intention setting is the act of focusing your RAS on that which *you* decide is important. And if you don't decide what's important, your brain will go into random selection and make choices based upon your mood, emotional state, and energy levels, which can fluctuate at any given moment. Without setting an intention, the brain operates in *default mode*, which is especially dangerous for those of us who have grown up in the struggle, because often those repetitive default settings are what cause us to internalize oppression and sabotage ourselves over and over again.

Default mode keeps you stagnant. Default mode keeps you stuck in the same routines, eating the same foods, engaging in the same habits, and repeating the same toxic cycles that have diverted your growth all along. Default mode is the system that has held us back for generations.

Eva taught me an analogy that illustrates the power of intention perfectly. Imagine that your brain is a highly trained search-and-rescue dog with the incredible ability to pick up scent from miles away. In movies, they often send rescue dogs into the wilderness to save a missing person—the dogs run through the forest, tracing the person's scent so they can bring them back to safety. But what's the first and most vital step that happens before the dogs are released into the wild?

They must be given the original scent.

Without the original scent—*the intention*—the dogs would aimlessly chase every distraction that peaked their interest. They would stop at every tree or go off chasing a squirrel when they were supposed to be saving someone.

Not setting intentions is like sending your brain into the forest of your life without giving it a guiding scent to follow. Many of us live life this way and wonder why things never seem to fall into place.

Intention is much more than just a dedication or a purpose; it is our way of giving the universe direction. If we are not clear about our intention, our outcomes will be scattered, and our brains will go barking up every tree. Without intention, every opportunity looks like a good opportunity. Without intention, you'll run around enjoying things momentarily until the next distraction comes. Without intention, your brain will stay in default mode, discarding valuable information needed for your growth while focusing on useless noise just because it's familiar.

Setting an intention is revolutionary. It gives you the power of choice and tunes your RAS to focus on information that will lead you to the life you most desire.

So here's the million-dollar question: *WHAT is your intention?*

That's where writing a vision comes in.

I'm going to walk you step by step through the process of writing your vision. Be sure to read to the very end of this chapter before you start writing. Even if you've written a vision before, don't skip ahead, because this process is going to be a little different than you might expect. At the end of this chapter, you'll have five blank pages on which to write your vision. For now . . . just keep reading.

IF YOU NEVER THINK BEYOND YOUR CURRENT CIRCUMSTANCES, HOW CAN YOU EVER LIVE BEYOND THEM?

When I'm working with clients, I'll often say, "Imagine you can rub a magic lamp. All things are possible, and everything you could ever wish for is at your fingertips. Then what?" That's where a powerful vision is birthed from.

I want your vision to be BIG—even bigger than feels comfortable.

You want your vision statement to sound so incredible that you become filled with excitement every time you read it—so much excitement that if your vision actually came true, it would feel like a miracle.

This might seem uncomfortable to you. It might feel silly or impossible. Good. I want to decondition your mind from lack and limitation. **If you never think beyond your current circumstances, how can you ever live beyond them?**

For most of us, there is a paradox of sorts between the life we're living now and the life we dream of. It's hard to believe that our current circumstances could ever lead to our limitless potential. That's why writing a vision is so important. It tunes your RAS to focus on hope and possibility, and it asks you to imagine a brighter future beyond your current circumstances, bringing a greater sense of alignment and resonance between your *real life* and your *dream life*.

WHAT YOUR VISION AND WAKANDA HAVE IN COMMON

When Ryan Coogler signed on to direct the *Black Panther* movie, he had never even been to Africa. Coogler could have disqualified himself because of this, but instead he saw that limitation as an opportunity. How could he learn more? How could he grow? How could he create a vision beyond his scope of reference? All this exploration led to a vision of the Afrofuturistic country we all know as Wakanda. Wakanda represents, among many things, a place inside each of us that holds the most valuable treasures of our life—the jewels, the vibranium, the unique gifts we are meant to share with the world. But to common folk, Wakanda is invisible, a fantasy that can't be located on a map. To get inside this kingdom, you need a secret code. This code is not spoken nor pronounced—it is a subtle vibrational energy that breaks through even the most powerful walls of protection.

Wakanda is the vision. *Meditation is the secret code that gets you there.* It will disarm your age-old defense mechanisms. It will break down your invisible force field, the one you created to protect you from your trauma. It will heal your wounds. It will bring you into greater alignment. It will help you *become* your Highest Self so you can claim your rightful seat on the throne.

I want you to really think about this. Wakanda was just an idea, a vision in someone's mind. It has now become a symbol of unity and pride for black people around the world. It gives us something to aspire to, something to dream for, and something to work toward. Coogler's vision broke box-office records, but most importantly, it evoked a new consciousness that inspires us to reimagine what's possible.

THE MOST POWERFUL VISION OF ALL TIME

All of the most successful people in the world understand the importance of a big vision.

Here's one that you've likely heard before—one that I believe is the most powerful vision of all time: Martin Luther King Jr.'s "I Have a Dream" speech.[2]

Here are some of my favorite excerpts:

Go back to Mississippi, go back to Alabama, go back to South Carolina, go back to Georgia, go back to Louisiana, go back to the slums and ghettos of our northern cities, knowing that somehow this situation can and will be changed. Let us not wallow in the valley of despair.

So I say to you today, my friends, that even though we face the difficulties of today and tomorrow, I still have a dream. It is a dream deeply rooted in the American dream.

I have a dream that one day this nation will rise up and live out the true meaning of its creed: "We hold these truths to be self-evident: that all men are created equal."

I have a dream that one day on the red hills of Georgia the sons of former slaves and the sons of former slave owners will be able to sit down together at the table of brotherhood. . . .

I have a dream that my four little children will one day live in a nation where they will not be judged by the color of their skin but by the content of their character.

I have a *dream* today. . . .

And when we allow freedom to ring, when we let it ring from every village and every hamlet, from every state and every city, we will be able to speed up that day when all of God's children—black men and white men, Jews and Gentiles, Catholics and Protestants—will be able to join hands and sing in the words of the old Negro spiritual, "Free at last! Free at last! Thank God Almighty, we are free at last!"

That is a vision.

When you write your vision (but not yet—keep reading!), I want you to imagine that you are writing your own "I Have a Dream" speech. One that goes beyond your current circumstances. One that ignites a fire in your spirit. One that inspires awe and gratitude. One that aligns you with a mission and maps out a route that your RAS can follow. It's time to dream BIG.

SETTING BIG GOALS WITHOUT GETTING DISAPPOINTED

I already know what you're thinking: "But how can I write such a big vision without setting myself up for disappointment?"

Remember this: **Your vision is not about accomplishing a goal. It's about who you become in pursuit of that vision.**

So don't worry about your vision being "realistic." Don't worry about it manifesting exactly as you see it, because it usually doesn't. Visions almost always manifest differently (and sometimes better) than you expect. If you feel disappointment, be compassionate with yourself and remember there's no such thing as failure. There are only lessons. Every time we fall off track or turn down the wrong road, we get feedback—and we need feedback to grow.

YOUR VISION IS NOT
ABOUT ACCOMPLISHING
A GOAL. IT'S ABOUT
WHO YOU BECOME
IN PURSUIT OF THAT VISION.

THE 5 LIFE ZONES: THE SECRETS TO WRITING THE ULTIMATE VISION FOR YOUR LIFE

Here's what I want you to do. Pretend you could get into a time machine, travel twelve months into the future, and write your vision *as if it had already happened*. Think of your vision as a thank-you note to life, the universe, God, or whatever Higher Power you believe in for all of the incredible things that will transpire in your life.

For example, "Thank you so much, universe, for my incredible interview with Oprah this year. Our connection was so natural, flowing, and easy. It's like we were old friends! I'm so grateful that our interview is being seen and heard by millions of people around the world, reminding them that they are worthy, they are powerful, they are ready, and they deserve the life of their dreams. Oprah and I even got to meditate together before the show. It was magic." (Yes, that's actually in my personal vision!)

I have provided blank space at the end of this chapter for you to write about each of these 5 Life Zones: Work, Passions, Wellbeing, Relationships, and Finances. Focusing on each zone individually is the best way to make the most of your vision.

I know you're probably tempted to start writing now, but hang tight. Keep reading until I say, "Go!"

LIFE ZONE 1: WORK AND CAREER

What are you doing for work? Do you have a side hustle? How much time do you spend working? Do you travel for work? Did you change jobs? Did you start a business? Did you get a promotion? Talk about everything related to work here.

JORDAN is on a deep search for purpose and meaning, but he is hesitant to work on this section because he's afraid his goal isn't "realistic." Remember, a vision is *not* about being realistic. I encouraged him to imagine what his life could be like if he wasn't so worried about money, loans, and all the steps to accomplish his goals. Then what? Jordan's answer was clear: he wants to work in transitional justice, a field that provides reparations for people who have gone through large-scale human rights violations and social injustices. He did an internship for it in college and loved it, but he always gets overwhelmed by how few job opportunities exist and how much work (and time) it would take for him to get a good job in that field. For now, I advised him not to worry about all the steps—a vision is not the same as goal setting. The point is to give yourself permission to name what you *really* desire so your RAS can help you get there.

LIFE ZONE 2: CREATIVITY, PASSIONS, AND HOBBIES

I hear a lot of people say, "Oh, you should be making money doing something you love. Your job should be your passion." Although that is one possible vision, I don't believe it's the only one. It's completely legit to work a job just for money or to pursue a career for advancement.[3] You don't have to be working in the same field as your passion to find your work meaningful.[4] **Don't ruin your passion by trying to squeeze money out of something that is supposed to be casual fun.** If you have passion for dance, you might make your living working as a teller at a bank while joining the local hip-hop troupe on the weekends. The key is making dedicated space in your life for the things you love to do, even if they don't make you any money. What are you naturally interested in? What do you enjoy on your time off? Traveling? Astrology? Crystals? Video games? Learning Beyoncé choreo on YouTube? Write about what you love and how you can incorporate it into your life on a consistent basis. If you can't think of anything, write about something you've always been curious to learn.

AMBER loves going to Bible study. **JORDAN** is obsessed with dancing and working out. **LISA** is a yoga retreat fanatic, and **DAVID** loves acting, singing, writing, and performing.

Once you name your passions, be sure to fill in your vision with juicy details. How often do you engage with your passion, and where do you go to do it? How does it make you feel? Who is there with you? The more details, the better.

I know, I know. Your creativity is on fire, and you are ready to write. But I did not say, "Go" yet! Keep reading.

LIFE ZONE 3: PHYSICAL, EMOTIONAL, AND SPIRITUAL WELLBEING

What feeds your body, mind, and spirit? What are your self-care practices? Are you reading any books? Studying with any teachers? Learning a new spiritual practice? How many hours of sleep do you get every night? Are you on a specific diet? Are you working out? Doing yoga? Taking walks? Include things that you'll be doing twelve months from now to keep a positive mind-set, a healthy body, and a strong connection to your Highest Self.

AMBER, our busy mom, is having a hard time with this section because she can't imagine having enough time to practice self-care on a regular basis. I tell her to pretend she can have her best-case scenario. Even if she accomplishes only a few of the self-care items in her vision, it will still make her life light-years better than it is now. When I ask her, "What would feel so luxurious that it would recharge and rejuvenate you to be more fully present for your work and family?," Amber gets excited. Some of her ideas: taking a bath every night once everyone is asleep, having amazing, intimately connected sex with her husband at least three times a week, going on long walks on her lunch break while listening to motivational podcasts, and getting to spend quality time with her child every night.

LIFE ZONE 4: RELATIONSHIPS

Are you married? Monogamous? In an open relationship? Celibate? Single and flirty? Do you have kids? Other people you're responsible for taking care of? Write about your relationships with friends, coworkers, and business partners as well. Remember, this is a new vision, so you may need to describe people you've never met. And don't forget about the most important relationship of all: the one you have with yourself!

LISA is a sexual assault survivor with a lot of relationship trauma to heal, so this section is difficult for her. At first she writes, "I'm grateful that I don't argue with my dad about politics anymore and I've finally manifested a loving partner despite my sexual trauma." That's a heavy vision that focuses on the past instead of the future. I ask her to keep her vision clear of words that insinuate conflict and negative energy, the things she doesn't want, and instead focus on what she *does* want. Her new vision reads, "Thank you, universe, for the loving, accepting, and beautiful relationship I have with my dad. I'm so grateful for him and the strength of our connection. And WOW!! I'm so thankful to have met the partner of my dreams. He is caring, tender, understanding, and loves me for who I am." Word choice matters. Your relationship zone should feel light, inspiring, empowering, and positive.

LIFE ZONE 5: FINANCIAL FREEDOM

I want you to get specific here. Twelve months from now, how much money do you have in your checking account? How much do you have in your savings account? Are you saving for retirement? How much money do you make every month? Write a specific number that would give you the financial freedom to actually experience life the way you want to. Don't base this off of anyone else's expectations. Financial freedom is being able to do what you want without worrying about money, so what do you really want?

DAVID, our aspiring artist, jumps into this section without hesitation. He envisions making a baseline of $10,000 per month specifically from his work as an actor and writer and selling one of his screenplays for $50,000. He has money in a savings account and can invest in an IRA to plan for his future. He is grateful to be able to buy organic food, help his parents with their debt, buy gifts for his many lovers, and take people out on fancy dates in the city with ease. This is perfect.

WHY MOST VISION BOARDS DON'T WORK

You may be tempted to skimp on one of the 5 Life Zones while you write. Don't. You have to write about all five of them; otherwise you risk creating a life that's out of balance. I learned this when I was first taught about the power of visioning by my dear friend, coach, and leadership expert Karen Mozes. If you focus your vision only on work and money, you risk overworking yourself and allowing your health and relationships to fall apart. If you write a vision only about your dream partner, you risk losing yourself, your friends, and your passions because you haven't taken into consideration how the rest of your life will shift once you get into a relationship. I don't want that for you. As Karen taught me: a balanced vision leads to an integrated life.

THE MOST IMPORTANT THING TO KNOW
BEFORE YOU START WRITING . . .

As you write your vision, keep this question at the forefront of your mind: "How can my growth, success, and self-improvement benefit all beings?"

Instead of asking, "How can I get ahead?" ask, "How can I serve?" Replace "What's in it for me?" with "How can I be a vessel?" If you filter every single part of your vision through the intention of service, you'll have a better chance at manifesting it.

The universe is not interested in your selfish, ego-based desires. It doesn't mean that you can't be famous. It doesn't mean that you don't have goals. It doesn't mean that you don't buy fancy things. But your *why*—your intention—needs to come from a place of *service*.

Everything you could ever hope for—love, respect, admiration, loyalty, care, attention, validation, and being valued, listened to, and understood—all come from being of service.

Some people call it "God's work," some call it "a calling" or "dharma." But one thing that's been proven to me over and over is that when you shift from self to service, the universe rushes in to support you in manifesting your vision more quickly than you can imagine.

I'm not necessarily suggesting that you become a teacher or open a nonprofit, but I want you to think about *how engaging in what you love affects the world around you*. How can you use your talents, your skills, your desires, and all the things that you love to benefit everyone you come in contact with? How can you benefit your community? Your people? Your family? The planet? Everything you've ever dreamed of is birthed from this place.

I know what it's like to have dreams and goals without knowing how or where to start going after them. Writing a vision is your first step. Then we take action. Trust me, this will change everything for you. If this little boy who grew up in a small town with all the odds against him, surrounded by violence, addiction, and abuse, could make this happen, I know with certainty that you can, too. I used exactly the same system that I'm teaching you in this book to manifest the life I've always dreamed of, and so have thousands of my students from all over the world. Now it's your turn.

Okay:

How to Redefine Your Life
(No Matter What You've Been Through)

STEP 1   Centering intention: Put your phone on silent and close your eyes if you feel comfortable doing so. Place your right hand over your heart and your left hand over your navel. Take five deep breaths in through your nose and out through your mouth. While you breathe, repeat this centering intention: "I am worthy. I am ready. I am powerful. I deserve this life."

STEP 2   Open your eyes and begin writing. Here are some pointers:

- You can use your own notebook if you'd rather not write your vision on the pages provided.
- Start with whatever Life Zone comes up first in your mind.
- Write your vision as if you're twelve months into the future. Write it in the present tense, as if it's already happened.
- It doesn't matter how long your vision is, just make sure it's dripping with juicy details. I recommend writing between five and twenty ideas for each section.
- You can use bullet points or write in paragraphs—it doesn't matter.
- Every sentence of your vision should start with words of gratitude, like, "THANK YOU" or "I am so grateful that . . . ," et cetera.
- At the end of each Life Zone, write a few lines about how your vision correlates with the spirit of service.
- You have permission to edit your vision whenever you want. It's okay if you change your mind. It doesn't mean that you've failed.
- If you get stuck, go back to the breathing practice in step 1.

STEP 3   When you're done writing, put your vision somewhere special so you can refer to it when you get off track. I like to read mine every full moon. Your vision doesn't have to be top secret, but keep it sacred. Be sure to mark your calendar for one year from now so you can remember to review your vision and see how far you've come.

Remember, you can't do this wrong. Have fun.

WORK AND CAREER

I am so grateful that . . .

A **VISION** **IS NOT** **ABOUT BEING** **"REALISTIC."** **GIVE YOURSELF** **PERMISSION TO** **NAME WHAT** **YOU REALLY** **DESIRE.**

This vision inspires me to be of service because . . .

CREATIVITY, PASSIONS, AND HOBBIES

I am so grateful that . . .

How often do you engage with your passion? Where do you go to do it? How does it make you feel? Who is there with you? The more details, the better.

This vision inspires me to be of service because . . .

PHYSICAL, EMOTIONAL, AND SPIRITUAL WELLBEING

I am so grateful that . . .

What recharges and rejuvenates you so you can be more fully present for your life?

This vision inspires me to be of service because . . .

RELATIONSHIPS

I am so grateful that . . .

Focus your vision on what you want, not what you don't want. Keep it positive and empowering.

This vision inspires me to be of service because . . .

FINANCIAL FREEDOM

I am so grateful that . . .

WHAT DOES REAL FINANCIAL FREEDOM MEAN TO YOU? BE SPECIFIC.

This vision inspires me to be of service because . . .

Essential Points from This Chapter

- Your thoughts don't create your reality; reality is cocreated among all of us, in both thoughts and actions.

- The reticular activating system (RAS) helps your brain zero in on exactly what it's looking for all the time.

- Setting an intention and writing a vision tunes your RAS to create the life you most desire. Without setting intentions, your brain runs on default mode and keeps you stuck.

- When you write your vision, be sure to dream BIG, include lots of details, and break it down into these 5 Life Zones: Work, Passions, Wellbeing, Relationships, and Finances.

- Don't worry about your vision manifesting exactly as you wrote it. A vision is not about accomplishing a goal, but about who you become in the process.

- If you want to supercharge your vision, shift your focus from "How can I get ahead?" to "How can I serve?"

CHAPTER

3

we stop self-sabotage

YOU GET WHAT YOU
ARE,
NOT WHAT YOU
WANT.

My Baca was always meticulous about making sure everything was squeaky-clean before she started cooking. She would always warn us about how the toxic chemicals, poisons, and germs would get us sick if we didn't wash everything thoroughly. The next step of our recipe is a little like cleaning the junk off your life so you can be clear for meditation. Learning to meditate while still engaging in self-sabotaging behavior is like watering a garden full of weeds. We must clear some of your toxic patterns to create space for new growth in the garden of your life.

When my students come to me and say, "I wrote a vision, but it's not happening," I always tell them this: You get what you *are*, not what you *want*.

You have to *become* the person in your vision—in both *vibration* and *action*. And there's nothing that lowers your vibration more than engaging in toxic patterns.

This quote by Yung Pueblo says it perfectly: "It's the things you say *no* to that really show the commitment to your growth."[1]

We all know this to be true. Think about the moments in life—although they're often brief—when you've taken a break from all of your vices or when you don't have any unnecessary drama happening around you. Think about the times when you stopped Band-Aiding your problems with drugs, or sex, or food, or sugar, or coffee and actually allowed them to heal.

If you want to manifest the vision you wrote in the last chapter, you must start by recognizing all the ways in which *you are your own poison*—the behaviors that are sabotaging you without you even realizing it. There are four toxic ways that we tend to sabotage ourselves. In this chapter you will identify those toxic patterns and learn practical steps to let go of what drags you down every time you try to grow. Please be kind to yourself as you go through this process. We all have toxic habits, we all experience self-sabotage, and of course things happen in life that are out of our control. We are all cocreating this web of reality together. So don't beat yourself up about it.

The subsequent exercises will help you identify your toxic behaviors, raise your vibration, and take action to align with the universal flow of your life.

LEARNING TO
MEDITATE WHILE
STILL ENGAGING
IN TOXIC BEHAVIOR
IS LIKE WATERING
A GARDEN
**FULL OF
WEEDS.**

FOUR WAYS YOU MIGHT BE YOUR OWN POISON

There are four areas to focus on when identifying the self-sabotaging patterns keeping you stuck:

1 Toxic habits   3 Toxic thoughts
2 Toxic people   4 Toxic beliefs

Let's dive into each of them more deeply.

BREAKING FREE FROM TOXIC HABITS

If you're doing cocaine every night or getting blackout drunk on the weekends, you don't need a book to tell you you're engaging in toxic behavior. The kind of toxic habits I want to help you identify in this chapter are a bit sneakier. They mask themselves as "normal," things that "everyone else is doing." These masked toxic habits are the most dangerous because they get invited into our lives, conversations, and routines and often become a part of our identity.

I define a toxic habit as anything you're engaging in regularly that lowers your vibration or keeps you from reaching your goals. That means a particular habit can be toxic now but become nontoxic later. Or it can be toxic for you, but not for your friends. Let me give you a personal example.

I've spent the last few years cleansing myself of my toxic habits to become as aligned as I can be with my intentions. I've given up porn, stopped drinking alcohol, stopped smoking weed, stopped drinking caffeine. I thought I had cleared all of my vices. But I was wrong. One day I went to my favorite intuitive counselor, a soulful, magical woman named Brenda Villa, to get a tarot card reading. And in that reading, she told me that I hadn't taken time to consider one of my most distracting habits.

Sex.

As soon as she said it, I knew she was right, because the idea of celibacy had been popping up in my meditations regularly . . . but I always ignored it. You have to understand: I'm a thirty-something, mostly gay single guy living in Hollywood, so giving up sex is kind of a big deal. Any time I even entertained the idea of celibacy, I always convinced myself that it wasn't necessary. Plus it was fun seeing my life play out like an episode of *Sex and the City* or *Noah's Arc*. When I talked to friends about it, they always advised me with confidence that I was *supposed* to be having lots of sex. After all, it's a defining part of your twenties and thirties. They were all watching porn, swiping through hookup apps, engaging in open relationships, and having one-night stands. Everyone and everything around me reinforced the idea that I should keep having sex, because it's normal, because it's connection, because "How could it be a bad thing?" Right?

Wrong.

Don't get it twisted—I don't believe sex is inherently bad or toxic. Sex is beautiful. It's one of the deepest forms of human connection. It's creation and passion. But if I'm being totally honest with myself, sex has often been one of my biggest distractions.

I was using sex for validation. For power. To release anxiety. To feel less isolated. I was sometimes dating people I didn't even really like, because I was lonely. I was staying up late texting and sexting, only to end up tired the next day and unable to give my full energy to the things that really mattered. I would go to parties and events and spend my entire time talking to the hot guy with big lips instead of networking or enjoying the company of my friends.

It all made sense, given my history. When you grow up hiding in the closet and never being accepted for who you really are, you learn to look for external sources of validation and love. For me, it started in high school with the boys who showed me love in all my gayness. We would secretly hook up in the locker room or back seat of my car after band practice. And just like that, sex became my main mode of validation, a pattern that continued well into adulthood.

It was time for a hard reset.

So I did the unthinkable. I gave up all sexual activity (even kissing!) for nine months. And it was incredible. I accomplished more in those nine months than I did in the entire year prior. I learned to redirect my sexual energy toward my dreams and goals. I got a surge of creative power I didn't even know existed and suddenly had enough time to sleep eight hours every night. I was making better choices, my income increased by 25 percent, and, most significantly, I signed my first book deal and ended up writing the book you're reading now.

The break from this toxic cycle took the poison out of sex. It forced me to confront my trauma instead of running away from it, which is the only way to heal anything. Ultimately, it allowed me to reclaim my power, and reset and reengage in sexual activity from a place of deep intimacy and connection instead of being on the leash of my lust.

I'm sure by now you're thinking of your own toxic habits and patterns. Here are a few things your fellow workshop participants have identified.

JORDAN

- Social media: because it always makes him feel worse—especially when he's comparing himself to other people.[2]
- Watching TV: because it eats up his time and can become an excuse for not working on his goals.

DAVID

- Porn and hookup apps: because they're a time suck and can have severe negative benefits on the human psyche (we'll talk about that more in chapter 14).
- Drinking alcohol: because it makes him cloudy, wastes his money, and disconnects him from his creative power.

AMBER

- Always saying yes: because she never has time to take care of herself.
- Gossiping (even with her close friends): because it trains her to always see the worst in people.

LISA

- Drinking coffee: because it becomes a crutch that always keeps her seeming "happy" and "energized" instead of processing her real emotions.
- Staying up too late too often: because she ends up tired, irritable, and unproductive the next day, and it feeds her caffeine addiction.[3]

Remember, none of these things are inherently bad. For some people, having coffee every morning or a glass of wine every night actually helps them find alignment. You have to decide what's right for you.

Pro tip: Use the vision you wrote in the last chapter as a litmus test to help you decide which habits you need to release. It's easy if you filter everything through this question: *Is the habit in question taking you closer to your vision or further away?*

What does the person you are in your vision do every morning? What kinds of conversations are you having with your friends? What do you do for fun? What do you watch on TV? How many hours are you sleeping? What are you eating? Who are you spending your time with? What do you need to release to become *that person*? It can be a sobering reality to face, but if you want to create meaningful change in your life, you must make new choices. You may need to let go of some of the habits you've had for a long time. The old you must die for the new you to be born.

THE OLD YOU MUST
DIE FOR THE
NEW YOU
TO BE BORN.

Toxic Habits: Breaking Free for Good

STEP 1   Centering intention: Place your hands over your heart, close your eyes, and imagine the version of you in your vision. Then take five deep breaths, and finish this sentence stem: "A habit that is pulling me out of alignment is _____." Repeat this process one to three times to identify as many toxic habits as you can. Write your responses in the first column of the grid provided.

STEP 2   In the second column, write some notes about why these habits are toxic for you. You'll need these as a reminder when the habits try to creep back in.

STEP 3   In the third column, identify new habits to replace the toxic ones. We often give up one vice only to replace it with another, so instead pick something that will make a positive impact on your life.

STEP 4   In the final column, make a clear time commitment for how long you plan to release this habit. Think of it as an experiment. At the end of your commitment, evaluate to see if and how you want to reintegrate this habit into your life from a more aligned state. Some habits might stay gone forever, but it's good to give yourself the option to check in and change your mind after a specific date.

Your classmate David has filled in the first row as an example.

Toxic habit	Why is it toxic?	What is a new habit you could replace it with?	For how long do you commit to releasing this habit?
Drinking alcohol	I waste money that I could be spending on something more important. I make bad decisions. Stay up too late. It makes me even more tired and depressed.	Instead of going to bars, I can save that money and invite friends over to watch movies. There's a huge list of movies I've always wanted to see, and it'll help me bond with my close friends more.	Two months

SETTING BOUNDARIES WITH TOXIC FRIENDS AND FAMILY

We've all heard about the importance of cutting toxic people out of our lives. But there's one kind of toxic person who often slips under the radar and yet is the most poisonous of all. I call this person the Skeptical Friend.

Seven Telltale Signs of a Skeptical Friend

1 When you share exciting news with them, you're not sure if they're happy for you or if they're jealous.

2 You sometimes hang out with them out of obligation. You don't really want to call or invite them, but you do anyway because you're afraid they'll get mad if you don't.

3 Your intuition knows something is a little "off" about this person, but you can't quite figure out what it is, so you ignore it.

4 They are passive-aggressive.

5 Sometimes you have to question whether they are mad at you or not.

6 You always find yourself walking on eggshells around them to avoid potential conflict.

7 They take pride in playing devil's advocate anytime you have new ideas.

Skeptical Friends are the most toxic people to have around you because they will subtly sabotage your success without you even knowing it. They're allowed into your life, your space, your home, your family, and they're allowed to hear about your dreams, goals, and aspirations. And when you're talking about your dreams and goals, sometimes all it takes is one pessimistic comment to take you completely off track.

I'm sure you're already thinking of somebody who fits this description, right? That little whisper in your mind is your gut instinct trying to give you a clue.

So what do you do?

If the person you're thinking about is somebody you can completely distance yourself from, *immediately* take steps to create space. As you begin to distance yourself, however, your Skeptical Friend might start texting you and asking, "Is there something wrong? It seems like you're being different." That's actually the point. You *are* being different. So don't get cold feet when they call you out for it. You have to set a boundary and hold your ground. If it would be productive to have an openhearted conversation to explain what's going on, fine, do that, but don't expect them to understand or take responsibility. In all cases, you must start protecting your energy from skeptical friends now.

Important note: I'm not suggesting that you cut everybody out of your life completely. If the Skeptical Friend you've identified is a family member or someone you cannot create permanent distance from, here's my golden rule: *Limit what you share with them.*

Maybe your mom is skeptical when you talk to her about your love life but not about your work. Or your best friend is skeptical when you talk about your creative ideas but gives great relationship advice. In those cases, you may just need to draw a circle around certain areas of your life and set a boundary.

It's okay to move in silence to protect your vibe.

Another important note about toxic loved ones: just because you identify someone as a Skeptical Friend *doesn't mean they're a bad person.* It doesn't mean you don't love them or care about them or that you have to cut them out of your life forever. This exercise is less about labeling people as "good" or "bad" and more about you setting healthy boundaries with people so that you can have a more elevated relationship with them and, most importantly, with yourself.

Remember, *you get what you are, not what you want.* The people you spend your time with are the greatest indicator of who you will become, so you may need to shift some relationships and friendships you've had your entire life. Do this exercise with compassion.

IT'S OK TO MOVE IN SILENCE TO PROTECT YOUR VIBE.

Toxic People: Setting Better Boundaries

STEP 1   Centering intention: Place one hand over your heart and the other hand over your navel. Close your eyes, take five deep breaths, and finish this sentence stem: "A person I need to create better boundaries with is

_____." Repeat this process one to three times to identify your Skeptical Friends. Write their names in column 1 of the grid provided.

STEP 2   In the second column, write the reasons you need to create distance from these people or topics you should limit sharing with them. You'll need this as a reminder when you find yourself tempted to abandon your boundaries.

STEP 3   In the third column, pick someone you could spend time with instead of your Skeptical Friend. Choose someone who uplifts and inspires you or someone whom you want to cultivate a deeper relationship with.

Lisa is being vulnerable and sharing her most challenging Skeptical Friend in the first row as an example.

if this work is triggering for you—that is, if you're starting to obsessively think about stuff, worrying about hurting people's feelings, your heart rate is rising, or you're tempted to put this book down because the work is too deep—I have something special for you.

Use this quick and easy breathing technique to regulate your nervous system. It's called the STFU Breath. It's simple:

STEP 1   Close your eyes if you feel comfortable doing so.
STEP 2   Inhale for 6 slow counts.
STEP 3   Exhale while making a long "shhhhhh" sound, like you're telling someone to be quiet. Try to make your exhale last for 20–30 seconds. Make it as long and slow as you possibly can.

Repeat two more times. Then pause, notice how you feel, and continue reading.

You can come back to this technique anytime you feel triggered. We'll talk more about the power of the breath in chapter 4.

Skeptical Friend	Why they are toxic?	Another person I could spend time with instead
My dad.	He thinks my personal growth is a waste of time and money. Every time I talk to him about privilege and social justice, he thinks I'm making a big deal about it and makes me question myself.	There's an amazing Native activist and musician I just met named Raye Zaragoza. I love her energy and want to build a relationship with her to learn more about what's important to the Native people of our country. I'm going to give her a call.

HEALING FROM YOUR TOXIC THOUGHTS

"I'm not good enough."

"I'll do it once I lose this weight."

"My parents would freak out if I did that."

"I wish I would've started when I was younger."

"I'm a fraud."

"People think I have my shit together, but I'm really a hot mess."

"Why am I so bad with money?"

Those are some of the most common toxic thoughts I hear from people. Toxic thoughts are the limiting beliefs and mind loops that make you second-guess yourself. When glossed over, these thoughts will ruin your life without you even noticing. But when you become aware of your toxic thoughts, you can catch them before they influence your actions.

We all have toxic thoughts, so don't be too hard on yourself as you identify yours.

The toxic thought that has negatively impacted my life most is: "My voice isn't good enough."

I know this might come as a surprise to you, since I've built my entire career around my voice, but it wasn't always that way. The attack on my voice began at a very young age. As soon as I started school, it become painfully obvious that something was "different" about the way I spoke. Apparently I talked "like a fag," and even though I had no idea what a fag was when I was eight years old, I knew I needed to talk differently to avoid being teased and beaten up. Unfortunately, I never got good enough at faking it, so the ridicule continued through high school.

Picture this. It's a Wednesday afternoon, and I'm standing in choir rehearsal with my entire second-grade class. In this particular class, we are preparing for our yearly recital, and our choir instructor, Ms. Bryant, is looking for someone to sing the solo part to a hit single that is hot on the charts that year.

When she asks for a volunteer, I immediately shoot my arm up into the air. I am so excited. I love singing so much that I spend most days after school singing in my room. I know this is a moment that I'll be able to shine. This is the moment I'll finally be praised for my voice instead of being teased about it.

So there I am, standing on the choir stand, surrounded by the entire class, including some of the most cruel bullies in the school, and for the first time ever, I sing to them. As soon as I open my mouth, the bullies go wild. They laugh, jump off the choir stands, and flick my ears from behind. And because bullies control everything when you're in the second grade, the rest of the class follows suit. The laughter echoes through the choir room, and I stand there in shock, trembling but afraid to cry, because, well, "only faggots cry."

It was in that moment that I shut down my voice.

I knew right then, at eight years old, staring at my feet while the entire class mocked me, that something I loved so much, something that brought me so much joy, something so authentic to me, was simply not good enough. It was something to be embarrassed about.

That's where my toxic inner voice was born. When I shut down my voice, I shut down my authenticity. I spent my entire childhood hiding in the dark, trying to pretend to be "one of the boys," meticulously monitoring how I walked, how I ate, whom I hung out with, and how high my voice was. This story had such a profound impact on my life that, to this day, I tremble a bit every time I retell it in front of an audience—and I've told it several hundred times at this point.

By now you're probably thinking of a story of your own—a time when you allowed someone to put a cap on your potential, to limit your power, or to make you believe that your dreams were better suited for somebody else. Our toxic thoughts often originate from trauma in early life. And although those traumas and situations are usually nonexistent in our current reality, we've internalized the hateful voices and learned to rerun an outdated script that was never ours to begin with.

Many self-help gurus will tell you to get rid of your toxic thoughts by drowning them out with positive affirmations. I don't know about you, but that shit never works for me. I can only repeat "I am beautiful" so many times in the mirror before I get bored.

I believe we must turn *toward* our toxic thoughts instead of trying to drown them out. I know that might sound crazy, but follow me on this one. When a toxic voice comes up, you have a choice. You can let it berate you and become paralyzed in fear, or you can learn why you've held on to this voice in the first place. You don't get rid of your toxic thoughts by sweeping them under the rug. You get rid of them by healing them at the root and then taking brave action to prove them wrong. This gives us a chance to take responsibility instead of being defined by the story our minds have invented. Your toxic thoughts are here to teach you something. They are a marker. An indicator. A flag in the ground pointing toward your growth and healing. I know it's not easy, but you must turn *toward* your toxic thoughts and listen to them with fierce self-compassion.[4] That's the only way they will ever stop running your life from the background.

Whenever you catch a toxic thought running wild in your mind, pause and ask this question: *In what area of my life do I need additional healing, support, or growth?* The answer to that question will give you a clue about where you need to invest additional time and energy to evolve beyond this toxic thought.

We'll walk through the process together in the next exercise.

Toxic Thoughts: Stopping Self-Criticism

STEP 1   Centering intention: Place your hands over your navel, close your eyes, take five deep breaths, and finish this sentence stem: "A limiting belief I have about myself is _____." Write down what you find in column 1 and repeat this process two more times until you discover three toxic thoughts.

STEP 2   Examine where the toxic thoughts originated. Did they come from a parent? Childhood trauma? An ex-lover? Write your answers in column 2.

STEP 3   What area of growth are your toxic thoughts pointing toward? In what area of life do you need additional healing, support, or growth? Maybe it's your confidence? Forgiveness? Self-love? Or a trauma that never had a chance to heal? Write your responses in column 3.

STEP 4   What is an action you can take to prove your toxic thought wrong? This might mean learning something new, committing to a practice, or moving out of your comfort zone. Remember, a baby step counts.

Please be compassionate with yourself as you go through this process. You are not doing it wrong, and you are not moving too slowly.

Amber has used the first row of the grid to tell us about a toxic thought shared by many women.

Toxic thought	Where did it originate?	In what area of life do you need additional healing, support, or growth?	What's an action I can take to prove it wrong?
I'm not a good enough mother.	I always promised myself my daughter would never have to grow up like I did, so when I yell at her or lose my cool, I feel like I'm failing.	I need to learn more ways to manage my stress. I'm sure there are many techniques and tools. I will search on Google.	Next time I feel like I'm going to snap, I will step away and use one of the Freedom Meditation breathing practices. It's better for me to step away than to react explosively.

DISMANTLING YOUR TOXIC BELIEFS

I used to be Mexican.

No, forreal, I was. Check this out . . .

My mom is adopted. When my grandparents picked my mom up from the hospital in the early 1960s, the doctors told them that she was Mexican. So I grew up identifying as half-black/half-Mexican for my entire life—so much so that my screen name on AOL Instant Messenger was bLaXiCAnbOi22. But it was a lie. The doctors were wrong. We did an Ancestry DNA test a few years ago and found out my mom is actually Persian and Middle Eastern. No Mexican at all. Yet I have danced in more than a dozen *quinceañeras, yo hablo español* almost fluently, and my mom can throw down on some *chorizo y huevos* better than any Mexican woman you've ever met.

This taught me one of my life's greatest lessons: our genetic makeup has nothing to do with our ability to love and embrace *all* cultures. Even with this new information about my identity, I don't feel any less Mexican than I did before. It all boils down to belief.

"Belief" is a powerful word—it holds more weight than "thought." Beliefs are the ideas you hold to be true about the world and your place in it. When you believe something, it creates a conviction in your spirit. Belief is what declares a guilty or innocent verdict in a trial. Belief is what causes people to come together and pray but also to kill, fight, and wage wars. If we are not careful about our beliefs, they can create massive separation, disintegration, and stuckness. Outdated beliefs and traditions often get passed down from generation to generation without anyone taking a moment to question whether or not they are still necessary or valid. When this happens, toxic beliefs keep entire communities stuck in an endless cycle of oppression.

Sometimes toxic beliefs are hard to identify. Here are some examples of the toxic beliefs plaguing your fellow workshop attendees.

LISA: "WE ARE ALL ONE."

We are not all one. And anyone who believes that we are needs to wake up from their peaceful, privileged slumber and come back to reality.

Yes, on a cellular level we are all made of the same stardust that creates the universe. Yes, I understand race is a construct that was created to make us forget we are all one human race that just happened to evolve differently on the basis of our geography. And yes, I believe we are all equally valuable and searching for the same sense of meaning and purpose regardless of our gender identity, race, creed, or economic standing. But as humans experiencing life on this planet, *we are not all one.*

If we actually want to see change on this planet, we must stop spiritually bypassing reality and, at the very least, acknowledge that we do not all have access to the same resources, opportunities, economic bounty, wellness, healthy food, and education. The more we keep perpetuating this idea that "we are all one," the easier it is for us to turn away from the places within ourselves and in our communities that need healing.

That homeless person you pass by on the street as if they were just a part of the landscape knows *we are not all one.* Jemel Roberson, the young black security guard who should've been considered a national hero for stopping a mass shooter at a bar but was instead killed by police when they arrived on the scene, knows *we are not all one.*[5] Those of us who worked our asses off to get into college while certain rich parents and their unqualified kids cheated their way through the admissions process know that *we are not all one.*[6] The people of Flint, Michigan, who lived without clean water for more than four years (and continue to live that way as I write this book) know that *we are not all one.*

If we really want true equality, we have to water our neighbors' gardens. We have to turn toward our differences and pour love, power, and justice into those places until they are flourishing. "We are all one" asserts that we are all the same. But thank goodness we're not; otherwise there would be nothing to learn. When we acknowledge our very real, and sometimes unfair, differences, we have two choices. We can build walls and call people "other," or we can look them in the eyes and ask, "How can I better understand you?" Don't ignore inequality just because it makes you uncomfortable. Otherwise you'll never be able to help.

> # THE PURSUIT AND GATHERING OF WEALTH IS NOT WHAT MAKES US GREEDY. IT IS **WHAT WE DO** WITH THE MONEY ONCE WE HAVE IT.

DAVID: "RICH PEOPLE ARE GREEDY."

No Bible verse was quoted more in my childhood than "It is easier for a camel to go through the eye of a needle than for a rich man to enter the kingdom of Heaven." Isn't that a convenient belief for Christian crusaders to have bestowed upon people of color when they came to rape, enslave, and colonize entire civilizations?

Every time I teach meditation, people resist talking about their desire for money because they're afraid it makes them seem greedy, or that money is not "spiritual enough" of a topic to focus on. The truth is, money is inherently spiritual because it reveals what we value and believe in.

My good friend and financial services guru Malcolm "MJ" Harris once said to me, "Money makes you more of who you already are. If you're a kind and giving person, it gives you more resources to give more. If you're an asshole, it gives you more resources to be an even bigger asshole."

The pursuit and gathering of wealth is not what makes us greedy. It is what we do with the money once we have it.

AMBER: "MONEY DOESN'T BUY HAPPINESS."

It actually does, but only up to a certain dollar amount.

I first learned this from my colleague and celebrity happiness coach Rob Mack. A 2010 study of Americans showed that people get noticeably happier with every dollar earned up to a threshold of $75,000.[7] Beyond that threshold, however, the level of happiness you get from every dollar decreases. For example, there's a substantial increase in happiness from $20,000 to $40,000, but not as significant of an increase from $1 million to $2 million. Put simply, you don't get as much bang for your buck after you're making enough money to pay all your bills and live comfortably without worrying.

While I think it's cool that they did a scientific study, people living under the poverty line have been trying to tell us this for years, but we've been busy believing the wrong narrative. We must stop shaming and guilting ourselves for the pursuit of wealth. Go secure your bags—it will make you happier.

JORDAN: "I NEVER GET ANGRY."

I used to be one of those people who bragged about "never being angry." Many of us are taught that anger is bad, which is understandable if you witnessed only unhealthy demonstrations of anger growing up, like I did. My primary examples of anger as a child were fighting, screaming, and abuse, so I vowed at a very young age that I would never be one of those toxic men who tore things down with their uncontrolled anger.

If you're a person who has trouble expressing anger or who thinks you are "more spiritual" because you never get mad about anything, I have some news for you: you're just experiencing yet another form of self-inflicted suppression disguised in a peaceful cloak. The most helpful lesson I've learned about anger was from author, integral psychotherapist, and spiritual teacher Robert Augustus Masters. He taught me the difference between anger and aggression and that it is just as important to be able to skillfully express anger as it is to express happiness, joy, and excitement. Healthy anger, always coupled with compassion and love, is what drives social justice movements and initiates change and growth. Aggression, on the other hand, only destroys. When we are aggressive, we hurt, belittle, and cross other people's boundaries. If you are striving for growth and change, you must practice the skillful expression—not suppression—of healthy anger.[8]

Here are a few more common toxic beliefs that you may want to consider:

- "#PositiveVibesOnly." That's exhausting. And fake. And causes people to vilify painful emotions that are worthy of being processed. Of course you want to be responsible for the energy you bring, but upholding a positive vibe all the time is phony and draining for you and everyone around you. Be real.

- "No pain, no gain." This insinuates that growth must always cause us harm. Not true. Stop saying it.

- "Only white people do that." I've heard this phrase my whole life, typically around things that are healthy for everyone, like hiking, yoga, meditating, eating organic food, using natural cleaning products and toiletries, caring deeply for nature, and reading instead of being glued to the TV. Honor your culture, but also pay attention to the things you label as "not for us."

- "It's better if I do it myself." This is a serious hurdle for conscious creatives and entrepreneurs, especially if you have lots of talents and skills and have been validated for overachieving. You must learn to ask for support.

- "You can love somebody only as much as you love yourself." LIES! The self-love myth says, "If you don't love yourself enough, then you'll never have real love." But, as I learned from my dear friend and love expert Arielle Ford, there's nothing more healing than being in a secure, loving relationship. Your imperfections will always be there. You'll always have room for growth. A loving partner can teach you how to love yourself despite all that.[9]

Hopefully those examples helped to attune your mind to the concept of toxic beliefs. Now it's time to explore some of your own.

Toxic Beliefs: Facing the Truth

STEP 1   Centering intention: Place your hands over your heart, take five deep breaths, and complete these sentence stems about the 5 Life Zones we identified in your vision:

"A toxic belief I have about my career that's holding me back is _____."

"A toxic belief I have about my passions that's holding me back is _____."

"A toxic belief I have about my wellbeing that's holding me back is _____."

"A toxic belief I have about relationships that's holding me back is _____."

"A toxic belief I have about money that's holding me back is _____."

You may not discover a toxic belief in each Life Zone. If you're having trouble differentiating between toxic thoughts and toxic beliefs, use this loose rule: toxic thoughts are about you; toxic beliefs are generally about life, the world, and your place in it.

STEP 2   Examine where each of your toxic beliefs originated. Was it from a family member? A social group? Religious organization? Write your answers in column 3.

STEP 3   How do these beliefs affect your life? Do they impact your experience of self? Of others? Do they cause fear? Arrogance? Belonging? Investigate to see if your beliefs are actually useful and true—or if they are just holding you back.

Jordan has absorbed a toxic belief that could keep him from pursuing his dream job. Now that he has identified it, he can consciously choose how he relates to it.

Area of life	Toxic belief	Where did it originate?	How does it affect your life?
Work and career	There aren't enough jobs in the field I want to work in.	My internship boss telling me how hard it was for her to get her job.	I don't even try because I think it's going to be too difficult, but just because it was difficult for my boss doesn't mean it will be the same for me.
Work and career			
Creativity, passions, and hobbies			
Physical, emotional, and spiritual wellness			
Relationships			
Financial freedom			

Essential Points from This Chapter

- There are four ways you might be sabotaging yourself without even knowing it: toxic habits, toxic people, toxic thoughts, and toxic beliefs.

- Learning to meditate while still engaging in toxic behavior is like watering a garden full of weeds. If you work toward clearing your toxic patterns, your vision will manifest faster.

- You get what you *are*, not what you *want*.

- When new forms of self-sabotage arise, you can always come back to these guided practices to help yourself through.

- Be compassionate with yourself as you identify and heal your toxic patterns. We all have them. It takes time.

CHAPTER

4

WE CHILL THE F*CK OUT

Wh-----en I first started learning to cook, I was surprised to learn that most all of my Baca's recipes started with the same three ingredients, celery, bell pepper, and onion—also known as the Holy Trinity of Cajun cooking.

Every cuisine around the globe has its own Holy Trinity, a simple three-part base that sets the flavor profile. Some of my favorites:

- Italian: tomato, garlic, and basil
- Chinese: green onions, ginger, and garlic
- Thai: basil, ginger, and lemongrass

But there's no trinity I love more than the **Freedom Trinity**—body, eyes, and breath.

What you do with your body, eyes, and breath will make or break your meditation practice. Meditating without these three elements would be like trying to assemble Ikea furniture without any tools or instructions. The Freedom Trinity is the foundation of your practice.

Now, you might be thinking to yourself, "Uh-oh—here it comes! All those rules I've never been able to follow. I knew this meditation thing was not for me." Don't worry. The Freedom Trinity has lots of wiggle room and space for experimentation.

THE IDEA THAT YOU NEED TO BE SITTING STILL AND CROSS-

BODY

After my parents divorced, we would go to my dad's house on Monday, Wednesday, and every other weekend. My dad's house was the one place all of my siblings, half siblings, and stepsiblings could be together—so, as you can imagine with five-plus kids running around, things got a little crazy. Whenever we pushed playtime boundaries too far, my dad would yell a magic phrase that would get us in check instantly.

Dad's magic words: "Sit yo' ass down!"

As soon as my siblings and I heard that one line, we somehow went from wild frenzy to complete stillness in a split second.

Do you remember something like this from your childhood? If so, hear me now. I am not your dad, your mom, your babysitter, or your seventh-grade homeroom teacher. Meditation should feel like the opposite of getting in trouble when you were a kid. It should feel like the opposite of being restrained, the opposite of being on time-out, and the opposite of sitting in church. Most of us have been trained to sit in rigid discomfort—at school, at work, and at church. We must undo that pattern.

So step 1 to the Freedom Trinity is simple. **Sit yo' ass down** ... *but comfortably.*

Most people think that you must sit still on the ground with your legs crossed to meditate. And I can understand why: if you Google the word "meditation," the first hundred images you'll see are pictures of white folks on mountaintops in stretchy yoga pants sitting with their legs crossed and their hands on their knees. I've been doing yoga for more than twelve years now, and sitting on

LEGGED WHILE MEDITATING IS SIMPLY NOT TRUE.

GET COZY—BECAUSE IF THE BODY IS

the floor cross-legged is still one of the most uncomfortable positions I've ever been in. It hurts my back, and my legs go numb—it sucks. Even if you're in great physical shape, sitting cross-legged for extended periods of time is likely to be uncomfortable. If that's true for you, just don't do it. The idea that you need to be sitting still and cross-legged while meditating is simply not true.

The most important thing about your position during meditation is that your body be *totally at ease*. Sit however and wherever you want; just get comfortable so that your body can come to a place of rest.

This might seem obvious, but if your body is uncomfortable, your brain cannot relax. Just think about it. One of your brain's primary functions is to keep the body in a state of balance, so if your leg is falling asleep from sitting in some weird position, your brain will fire off incessant signals to make the body move. If you're sitting in meditation thinking, "Even though my leg is tingling, I must sit totally still right now because I'm meditating," then your brain is going to go into overdrive. It will call upon all of its forces to make you move. If you don't move, your brain will make you itch, or sneeze, or cough, or go to the bathroom—it will do whatever it takes until you get out of that uncomfortable position. Your brain is powerful, and it's always going to win. **Get cozy—because if the body is not comfortable, the mind cannot relax.**

DAVID, our budding creative, loves to meditate on the floor with his back up against his bed. Busy mama **AMBER** likes to meditate in the bathtub because it's the only place she can find peace. **JORDAN**, our young'un on the search for purpose, is a night owl, so he's going to try meditating on his bed. And **LISA**, the occasional yogini, likes to sit cross-legged outside on her patio, with a cushion under her butt and another supporting her back so that she is actually comfortable.

Take a second and practice right now. Get comfortable. I mean *really* comfortable. Let it feel luxurious. Even if that means you need to get up and move to another spot. It doesn't matter if you're in a chair, on the floor, in your car, on the couch, sitting cross-legged, kneeling on your knees, or if you just grab some pillows and prop your back up against the wall. Anything goes.

And remember, *anytime your body gets uncomfortable, you have permission to move.*

EYES

One of the things I notice most often while teaching meditation is the forceful way in which people shut their eyes. When I instruct people to "gently close your eyes," most folks squeeze their eyelids together too tightly. They often have furrowed brows and wrinkles all around their faces from such an unnatural rejection of the outside world. Remember, Freedom Meditation invites us to become more fully present to the world that we are a part of, so we must shut our eyes in way that feels relaxed, gentle, and—most importantly—natural.

HOW TO CLOSE YOUR EYES PROPERLY DURING MEDITATION

You know that feeling you get when you're dozing off to take a nap? Or when you're reading a book and you accidentally fall asleep? That's how I want you to close your eyes when you begin to meditate. It should mimic the experience of drifting off to a restful slumber—the eyelids gently and slowly meet in peaceful surrender.

CAN YOU MEDITATE WITH YOUR EYES OPEN?

I have a story about this. In my early days of meditating, I was attending a yoga retreat at Esalen, my favorite spiritual retreat center in Big Sur, California. Big

Sur is, in my opinion, one of the most beautiful and majestic places in the entire world. Picture this: a group of about fifty of us were sitting outside meditating on a bluff, positioned perfectly to witness an unobstructed view of the sun setting over the Pacific Ocean. It was one of those perfect sunsets, the sky turning a gradient of intense orange, pink, and purple. There were dolphins jumping out of the ocean and a family of whales spraying water out of their spouts. The view was like nothing I had ever seen before.

But everyone had their eyes closed. Except for me.

They all missed one of the most magical sunsets I've ever seen because people think they're "supposed to" meditate with their eyes closed.

That's not true. There are even some forms of meditation that are meant to be practiced with your eyes open.

In Freedom Meditation, you are free to experiment. If you're indoors, at home, or somewhere familiar, it will probably feel natural to close your eyes. If you're somewhere beautiful, however, especially in nature, for God's sake *open your eyes.* At least for a moment. Take in the beauty that surrounds you.

IN FREEDOM MEDITATION,

I would estimate that about 80 percent of the time I meditate with my eyes closed. But if I'm practicing somewhere other than my typical spot at home, I like to start with my eyes open. If I'm traveling in a new city, I'll let my peripheral vision expand to soak up the energy of my new environment. If I'm outdoors, I'll watch the shapes of the clouds rolling by, or I'll immerse myself in the vibrant detail of a single flower. Once I take it all in, I might close my eyes and then open them again a few minutes later. Sometimes I even keep my eyes open for the entire practice. You will find your own balance.

Throughout this book, I will often invite you to close your eyes. Please remember this is always an invitation, not a command. You have permission to keep them open whenever you want.

BREATH

Did you know that the quality of your breathing changes automatically according to your emotional state? If you're stressed, scared, or angry, your breathing rhythm will get short and rapid. If you're relaxed and at ease, your breaths will be slow and deep. Modern science has proven what ancient yogis have known all along: the breath is inextricably connected to the nervous system. Deep exhales activate the vagus nerve, which calms the heart, enables digestion, strengthens the immune system, and deepens our experience of compassion.[1]

YOU ARE FREE TO EXPERIMENT.

This gives us power. The average person takes about 16 breaths per minute. That's 960 breaths per hour and more than 23,000 breaths per day. That means we have 23,000 chances *every day* to take charge of our emotions and regulate our nervous systems by harnessing the power of the breath.

Although Freedom Meditation is not a breathing practice, taking a few deep breaths before you meditate will help you relax into meditation more easily. Before I meditate, I always take three long inhales through my nose and three exhales through my mouth. No matter what kind of craziness is going on in my day, taking those three breaths always brings me closer to center.

Moving forward, I will refer to the combination of the three parts discussed in this chapter—the body, eyes, and breath—as the Freedom Trinity.

BODY   Sit yo' ass down . . . comfortably.
EYES   Open or closed.
BREATH   Take a few deep breaths.

Let's put everything together.

The Freedom Trinity: Do This Every Time You Meditate

Time: Set a timer for 3 minutes, but feel free to sit longer if you want.

STEP 1: BODY   Find a comfortable place to sit. Remember you can move anytime you feel discomfort.

STEP 2: EYES   Start with your eyes open, then allow them to close like you're surrendering to a peaceful nap.

STEP 3: BREATH   Be generous with yourself and take three slow inhales through your nose, exhaling through your mouth. Feel free to make a sighing sound when you exhale.

STEP 4   Let your breath return to its normal rhythm and spend the next few moments in silence until the timer rings. Don't worry if your mind starts racing—we'll be taking care of that in the next chapter.

Essential Points from This Chapter

- You do not have to sit on the floor cross-legged to meditate.

- Get cozy, because if the body is not comfortable, the brain cannot relax.

- Close your eyes gently instead of forcing them shut.

- Always take a few deep breaths before you meditate.

- Start each practice with the Freedom Trinity:
  BODY   Sit yo' ass down . . . comfortably.
  EYES   Open or closed.
  BREATH   Take a few deep breaths.

CHAPTER

5

we free our minds

F reedom. That's what I always felt when I was learning to cook with my Baca. It was a safe space for me to play and explore and mess up without any fear of judgment or expectation. I want that for you, too. I want meditation to be a safe haven for you to welcome *all parts of you*—an inner sanctuary where you can let your freak flag fly and express your authentic truth without any demonization or self-criticism. I'll warn you now that this can be the most challenging part for people, especially since most of us have been conditioned to question, demonize, and push down our thoughts since childhood. I definitely had plenty of

ALL THOUGHTS ARE WELCOME.
ALL FEELINGS ARE HONORED.

practice at that. It makes me sad to think about all the energy I invested in hiding my truth when I was a child. Like many young gay kids, I had an entire alternate life that I was concealing from my friends and family.

I remember a guy I was dating in high school who, for the sake of this book, we'll call "Ricky." Ricky was one of the most popular guys in school, and I was class president and captain of the drum line. We had a blossoming, deep love affair, yet neither of us was out of the closet, so we went to incredible lengths to hide our relationship.

Picture this. It's five o'clock in the afternoon, and band practice is just ending. All of my friends want to go eat at Denny's, but I tell them I can't because "my mom wants me to go straight home." So I hop into my green 1994 Mustang, pop the radio face back on to the dash, slip in my *The Emancipation of Mimi* CD, and drive away. A few minutes later, I pull off onto a random residential street where no one will find me and call my mom. I tell her, "I'm headed to Rita's house to do homework." "Okay," she says, "just be home by eight." I quickly send Rita a text message saying, "If my mom calls, don't answer. I'm gonna hang out with this girl I met at the movies." Then Ricky pulls up beside me and gets into my car. We lock hands. He reclines his seat so that no one sees him through the passenger window as we drive to an old, abandoned parking lot down at the marina where we can be all alone. That was always our spot. For the next two hours, we are free. The steam that covers the windows is like a fog of protection, insulating us from the harsh and judgmental outside world. It is our safe space. Everything is allowed, embraced, caressed, and loved.

ALL GUARDS ARE DOWN.

I want your Freedom Meditation practice to feel like the inside of that old 1994 Mustang. No boundaries, no judgments. All thoughts are welcome, all feelings are honored, all guards are down. Let's put that into practice now.

The goal of this practice is simple: *to notice the thoughts coming and going in your mind and to welcome them without judgment.* Give yourself permission to welcome every single thought that comes—and not just the "good" ones. Even thoughts about death, violence, war, porn, or anything that feels incestuous, wrong, or dirty. Don't push anything down. Suppression is proven to have major consequences on your physical health and emotional wellbeing.[1] Also welcome your spiritual positive thoughts, random colors and images, Mariah Carey song lyrics, et cetera. Everything is fair game. Give yourself freedom to play, just like my Baca gave me in the kitchen.

WELCOME

Stop Pushing Down Your Thoughts

Time: 3 minutes

STEP 1   Start with the Freedom Trinity we created in the last chapter. Find a cozy way to sit, engage your eyes, and take a few deep breaths, exhaling with a sigh through your mouth.

STEP 2   Let your mind run wild. Give yourself full permission to let it go crazy. Don't try to control anything. Most of us oscillate between pushing down our thoughts and ignoring them completely. This practice is offering a third option: *welcoming*.

STEP 3   After the timer rings, immediately write down everything you can remember thinking about during the 3 minutes. It's okay if you don't remember it all.

> Go ahead, try it now.

If your thought patterns were all over the place, you're doing this right. I'm giving you full permission to just let your mind run wild. In the next chapter, I will teach you how to anchor your thoughts, because meditating and daydreaming are not the same thing. But before you can learn to anchor your thoughts, you have to learn to welcome them without beating yourself up about it.

Here's what some of your fellow workshop participants thought about.

DAVID   "I thought about sex. But then I started judging myself because I knew I was going to have to write it down, so that led me to thinking about the judgments I have about sex. And then I told myself, 'You should stop thinking

EVERYTHING.

about sex.' Then I started thinking about how my parents immigrated to the US and how hard it was for them. I just want to make them proud."

LISA   "I was thinking about flights. I have some trips I need to book, and I was getting worried that prices are going up. And then I imagined the plane crashing, but that scared me . . . then all of a sudden I started hearing Beyoncé singing that song about hot sauce and surfboards."

AMBER   "All I could think about was my kids and what I should make for dinner."

JORDAN   "I kept thinking about my sister and all her drama. Her situation is really putting a strain on my family. I wanted to think about something positive, though, so I made myself think about my two best friends and how lucky I am to have them in my life."

Some of the most common thoughts that come up for people are:

- To-do lists.
- Sex.
- Creative ideas.
- Conversations with friends or family members.
- Their kids and fearful visions about how they might die.
- Unfinished business—things they forgot to do, people they need to talk to, conversations they never had, things they need to do later, or things they anticipate doing in the future.
- Family, song lyrics, random colors, movie scenes . . . the possibilities are endless.

Welcome everything.

THE SIX HIDDEN FORMS OF THOUGHT
AND WHY YOU SHOULD CARE

There are six ways we experience inner thoughts. I'd like to introduce you to the 6S Thought Spectrum:

1 Sights
2 Sounds
3 Smells

4 Snacks
5 Sensations
6 Sentiments

Let's break this down a bit further.

SIGHTS

When asked to think of an ocean, you see the waves crashing against the shore.

The first form of thought is *sights.* If you identify with this thought form, you experience thoughts as visuals—images or movies playing in your head. If you're thinking about your kids, you'll see their faces. If you're thinking about Burning Man, you'll visualize the playa—lights glowing, dust blowing, and art cars shooting fire.

SOUNDS

When asked to think of an ocean, you hear the sound of the waves.

The second form of thought is *sounds.* If you associate with this part of the spectrum, thoughts manifest in your mind as an auditory experience. You may hear your own voice or somebody else's voice talking as you think. People who identify with this thought form often hear music playing in their heads. If you're thinking about your mom, you'll hear her voice in your mind. If you imagine taking a flight, you'll hear the flight attendants talking over the intercom, the loud buzz of the airplane, and the *ding!* that happens every time the Fasten Seat Belt sign comes on.

SMELLS

When asked to think of an ocean, you smell the sand, water, and sunscreen.

Did you know that *smell* was the first sense developed by most living beings and is often the last sense we lose before we die? The sense of smell is also closely linked to memory recall, probably more so than any other sense. Think about it. If you smell a pumpkin spice latte in the summer, you'll be instantly transported into the fall. If you smell the cologne your ex-boyfriend used to wear, you immediately remember him, whether you like it or not. Smell is a powerful gateway into your internal world.

SNACKS

When asked to think of an ocean, you taste the salt water (or maybe even a piña colada).

Certain thoughts may activate your sense of *taste*.. If you identify with this thought form, thinking of dark chocolate, red wine, or mac 'n' cheese might make your mouth water as if you were actually consuming it. When I think of being at my Baca's house, I often taste her recipes on my tongue. Taste leaves an imprint that we can recall in an instant.

SENSATIONS

When asked to think of an ocean, you feel the cool water on your skin.

The fifth form of thought is grounded in your physical body and is all about a heightened awareness of your internal *sensations*. Certain thoughts might trigger aches and pains, while other thoughts may initiate a tingling or a buzzing sensation. If you identify with sensations, thinking about summer could activate a literal feeling of heat from the sun even if you're in the dead of winter.

SENTIMENTS

When asked to think of an ocean, you feel peaceful and relaxed.

If you identify with this form, specific thoughts cause a change in your emotional state. So you may think about your kids and get happy, or you might think about the biases in the criminal justice system and get angry. *Sentiments* are about your emotions and how thoughts cause them to shift.

Everybody experiences thought differently. You will identify with some forms more than with others. You might experience a single form or a combination of two or three forms at the same time. And although most people have an affinity to a specific thought form combination, where you land on the spectrum can change from day to day, so don't get attached to any specific thought form over another. I'll teach you how to identify yours in a moment.

WHY MOST GUIDED MEDITATIONS BECOME BORING AFTER A WHILE

I remember the very first time I ever tried to meditate. I was nineteen years old and attending UCLA, and I went to a yoga class at our gym. At the end of class, the teacher began to guide us through a meditation. In her artificially calm yoga-teacher voice, she instructed us to "close your eyes and imagine a river," so I sat there trying my best to make it happen. I didn't know it then, but sights weren't a form of thought that I identified with. Plus I had never even been to a river before, so trying to imagine one was tough. The teacher continued, "Imagine you see a boat on the river and you get inside the boat." I got really stressed because I still didn't see the river, and now she wanted me to imagine a boat! The instructions went on: "Imagine sitting inside the boat and beginning to paddle toward a beautiful sunset." I was done. I sat there for the next twenty minutes feeling frustrated and irritated, convinced meditation just wasn't for me. How was everyone else having such a deep experience when all I could think about was how hungry I was?

At the end of the class, the teacher asked me, "How was it?" Of course, I told her it was "incredible and life-changing," just like everyone else in the room did.

This is what happens to most of us during guided meditations. We spend so much energy trying to force ourselves to follow the instructions that often we lose touch with our natural, innate experience of thought. Guided meditations are useful, but they're like meditating with training wheels. There's a phrase in the tech world, "responsive design," which is a fancy way of saying a website will "respond" to the size of your screen. It's the reason some websites look different on your phone than they do on your computer. A responsive design adapts to your life—and that's what I believe is required for a lifelong meditation practice. As you continue to learn to meditate and engage with the guided meditations in this book, remember, you have permission to experience thought in six different ways: sights, sounds, smells, snacks, sensations, and sentiments.

The following practice will guide you through identifying which forms of thought you resonate with most.

Get Inside Your Own Head

Time: 3 minutes

STEP 1 Start with the Freedom Trinity.

STEP 2 **Think of a place you love**. It can be anywhere—just make sure it's a place that makes you feel good. As you call this place forth in your mind, explore it with wonder and in as much detail as possible.

STEP 3 After 3 minutes, write down which forms of thought you experienced most noticeably: sights, sounds, smells, snacks, sensations, or sentiments. Remember, it can be a combination of them.

Essential Points from This Chapter

- Welcome all of your thoughts during meditation—even the naughty ones.

- Try not to judge your thoughts as they arise.

- The 6S Thought Spectrum identifies 6 forms of thought:
  Sights   Snacks
  Sounds   Sensations
  Smells   Sentiments

- You may experience any combination of the 6 forms.

- Where you fall on the spectrum can change from day to day, so don't get attached.

CHAPTER

6

we got   the sauce

THE REAL POINT OF MEDITATION IS TO REALIZE **THE GURU** IS WITHIN YOU.

Everybody's favorite part of the Freedom Meditation recipe is the *secret sauce,* and we're about to create yours now! Your secret sauce is the special something that's going to make your recipe pop. It's the *unique energy signature* of your personal practice. I have only one rule when it comes to creating your secret sauce: it has to be infused with *your* natural essence. No one else's dogma or tradition is welcome here but your own.

One of the things I've always found odd about yoga and meditation is that people chant words in languages they don't understand and never stop to ask what the words even mean. If I'm being totally transparent, I need to say that I got sick of listening to American yoga teachers telling me to chant in Sanskrit (an ancient yogic language) when they couldn't even pronounce the words properly or explain the full definitions of them. Becky would tell me, "Don't worry about what it means," "Don't worry about saying it right," "You don't have to know where it comes from," or "Just feel it in your heart and experience the magic." Sounds like a classic recipe for cultural appropriation to me. And while I think it's great to enjoy practices from other cultures and traditions (like meditation), whispering a bunch of mispronounced gibberish with no reverence for the language just didn't feel right to me.

So I quit Sanskrit. But I was nervous. My meditation teacher Lorin has been immersed in the study of Sanskrit for more than forty years. How was I ever going to tell him that I was abandoning Sanskrit? There I was, twenty-five years old, sitting on the couch across from Lorin at his condo in Marina Del Rey, California, and I finally got the guts to say it. "Lorin, I fucking hate Sankrit! And I'm sick of all these yoga teachers telling me that I have to chant it to meditate when they don't even know what they're talking about."

His response? "Good. Fuck it!"

I was shocked. Here I was confessing my irritation with Sanskrit to a Sanskrit guru and he was telling me, "Fuck it"?

Lorin then said something that changed my perspective on meditation forever. "It's okay if you reject Sankrit. You don't have to accept any external guru. **The real point of meditation is to realize the guru is within you.**"

That was a game changer for me, and it solidified my deep love for the freedom of this style of meditation.

Over the years, I have healed my relationship with Sanskrit. I don't have anything against the language itself but, rather, with the careless use of something so sacred. Many people enjoy Sanskrit, and others prefer to experience meditation in their own native tongue. Both are fine, but if we choose to adopt a foreign culture's language for our meditation practice, we must also take the time to learn what the heck we're saying and honor where it comes from. In Freedom Meditation, we don't need a secret Sanskrit ingredient for the magic to happen. We cook up our own secret sauce. We become our own gurus. Here's how . . .

Important note: Don't skip ahead. It's crucial that you complete the following practice before you continue reading—otherwise you may miss out on the full experience.

Discover Your Unique Energy Signature

Note: if you prefer to be guided through the audio version of this special practice, listen at justinmichaelwilliams.com/staywoke.

STEP 1   After you read this paragraph, I want you to close your eyes and imagine a ball of energy in front of you. This ball of energy is your own personal source of power. It has the power to heal all of your pain, fix all of your problems, and bring you into full alignment with your Highest Self. It is unique to you and can be any color, any shape, and any size. It can be translucent, shimmery and sparkly, or dense and dark. There's no right or wrong way to imagine it. Remember, you don't have to visually see it to imagine it—use any of the six forms of thought. Take as much or as little time as you need to get a clear experience of the energy ball in your mind. Once you clearly sense the ball, open your eyes and move on to step 2. Go ahead, close your eyes and imagine the energy ball now.

STEP 2   Once you finish reading this paragraph, I want you to bring forth that same ball of energy, but this time, we're going to incorporate the breath. Take long, slow, deep breaths in through your mouth and out through your nose. On each inhale, pretend you're sucking in the essence of your energy ball, as if you're sucking through a straw. Have you ever seen the movie *Hocus Pocus*? The one starring Bette Midler? There's a scene in the movie where she and her sister witches suck the life-force out of the children of Salem to replenish their souls. That's what I want you to do with your energy ball. Replenish your spirit. If you haven't seen the movie, imagine you're sucking through a straw or inhaling through an asthma inhaler. Don't be afraid to make some noise while you do this. As you inhale through your mouth, imagine the energy entering your body. As you exhale through your nose, the energy spreads further and deeper through your system. Take several breaths. As you breathe, the ball continues to replenish itself with an endless source of energy. It's limitless. With each breath, the energy fills every crevice of your inner body with its magic. It's perfect for you. It fills you up like a gas tank with exactly what you need in your life right now.

Set a timer for 2 minutes and breathe in the energy of your ball until the timer rings. Go ahead, do it now. Then immediately move on to step 3.

STEP 3   Using one, two, or three words in the language of your choice, *name the type of energy your ball is made of.* What is it filling you up with? Go with the first answer that comes to your mind.

Note: Do not flip to the next page until you've answered the question.

WRITE THE WORDS THAT DESCRIBE YOUR ENERGY BALL BELOW:

Congratulations. **You just created your mantra.**

And I know you might be thinking, "OMG . . . no. It's not spiritual enough of a word" or "I'm not sure if this is the right thing." Don't worry, you can change it later. But before you second-guess yourself, let's clarify a few things, because your first answer is usually your natural intelligence identifying exactly what you need.

WHAT IS A MANTRA?

Most of us have heard the word "mantra" at some point in our lives, but do you actually know what the word means?

Let me tell you what a mantra is *not*:

It's not an affirmation.
It's not something you have to repeat.
It's doesn't have to be a word in a foreign language.
It doesn't have to be top secret.
It doesn't lose its power if you talk to people about it.
It doesn't have to be sung or chanted.
It doesn't need to be given to you by some guru or self-proclaimed spiritual master.

The word "mantra" actually comes from two different words in Sanskrit. ("But wait—doesn't Justin hate Sanskrit?" Nope. What I hate is the misuse and appropriation of the language without any reverence or context.) Let's break down "mantra" so you can experience its genius. *Man* means "thoughts." *Tra* means "a tool." When these words come together, we define *mantra* as "a tool of thought."

If you needed to hang up a picture frame, you would grab a hammer. If you needed to install curtains, you would grab a drill. If you need to fix something in your mind, you grab a mantra. A mantra will give your thoughts direction and purpose and help you anchor them so that they work for you instead of against you.

WHY IS IT IMPORTANT TO CREATE YOUR OWN MANTRA?

The first time I meditated with Lorin on the beach, he began guiding me through some simple breathing practices and visualizations. It all felt so easy and natural that I didn't even realize he was initiating me into meditation. Then, after about five minutes, he asked me this simple yet life-changing question: "If meditation could be about *one thing* for you—if it could bathe and soothe *exactly* what you needed all the time—what would it be?"

I responded immediately with two words: "COMPLETE AUTHENTICITY."

And, just like that, my first mantra was born.

Like I mentioned before, up until that point, I had been chanting only the basic affirmations and Sanskrit mantras my yoga teachers had given me. But I had never felt a sensation like the one I felt when the words "COMPLETE AUTHENTICITY" came roaring out of my mouth. I knew, in that moment, that I was home.

If I could truly cultivate those words . . .

"complete": total, full, and untarnished

"authenticity": living in my truth, expressing my full power, and never holding myself back

. . . then I would finally be able to step into a new chapter of my life. The shadows of my childhood—hiding myself, feeling unworthy, feeling like I didn't belong, priding myself on being a chameleon but losing myself in the process—had haunted me for most of my life. But with "COMPLETE AUTHENTICITY" as a mantra, maybe all of that could be healed.

And that's exactly what started to unfold for me. I stuck with that mantra every single day for two years as it slithered its way into the most hidden crevices of my being. It healed my wounded places. It ignited a spark in me that had been shut down from years of being called "too much," "too gay," "too feminine," and "too flamboyant." Within those two years I doubled my income, ended a relationship that wasn't right for me, reawakened my singing voice, and started building a totally new community of friends.

This is the power mantra—your new tool. One that has been uniquely designed and given to you by the natural intelligence of *your* Being.

Creating your own mantra allows you to feed the special need that's inside of you and fill yourself up with an energy that makes *you* feel good. It's the secret sauce that makes even the most bitter memories more digestible. This is how we turn meditation into a treat instead of a chore.

For the rest of this chapter, I'm going to guide you through building a relationship with your mantra and how to know if you need to change it to something else.

WHAT YOUR MANTRA AND A FIRST DATE HAVE IN COMMON

Your first experience with your mantra is kind of like a first date. You're hopeful but uncertain and maybe even a little afraid or resistant—tainted by past dating experiences. Some of the best dating advice also applies to your first practice of mantra:

- Be open to new experiences.
- Remember that expectations lead to disappointment.
- Spend more time listening than talking.

Aspiring artist **DAVID** is going on a date with his new mantra "Ray of the sun" because it gives him energy. **AMBER**, our busy mom, is using the mantra "Love." **JORDAN** is on the deep search for purpose and meaning, so he chose "Clarity and peace," and **LISA**'s mantra is "Salty rocks," because her most peaceful memory is sitting on salty rocks at the beach as a little girl watching her dad surf.

Some people like to keep it classy on first dates and try to take it slow. Don't do that with your mantra. I want you to *go all the way*. Test-drive this thang in every way possible so you can decide whether or not you want to continue building a relationship. There's nothing like going on five dates with someone only to find out they're a bad kisser.

I have eight techniques you can use to figure out if you're compatible with your mantra. I want you to explore all of these or any combination of them to see what works best for you. Read all eight options first. We will walk through them together in the next guided practice.

TECHNIQUE 1   Repeating the words of your mantra silently in your mind.

TECHNIQUE 2   Repeating the words of your mantra aloud.

TECHNIQUE 3   Repeating the words of your mantra in a quiet whisper.

TECHNIQUE 4   Repeating the words of your mantra slowly.

TECHNIQUE 5   Repeating the words of your mantra rapidly.

TECHNIQUE 6   Repeating your mantra in sync with the rhythm of your breath. Breathe in and breath out, with each word of your mantra attached to your breathing pattern.

TECHNIQUE 7   Repeating the words of your mantra just for a moment, but then allowing the words to transform into a sight, sound, smell, snack, sensation, or sentiment.

TECHNIQUE 8   Not using the words of your mantra at all, but instead returning to the energy ball technique, which I like to call your *Mantra Ball*. If you are a visual person, this technique may work well for you. Imagine your

PLAY AND EXPLORE WITH A SENSE OF WONDER.

COMMIT TO ONE MANTRA UNTIL YOUR SOUL KNOWS IT'S TIME TO MOVE ON.

mantra as an orb of energy. It can be multiple colors, iridescent, transparent, or solid—allow it to change and evolve naturally. Then play with that ball in your mind. Let it contract until it becomes so small you can hold it or expand so large that your entire body can drop into it. I like to imagine that I'm swimming in my Mantra Ball—floating inside it, like I'm underwater, totally surrounded in a bath of its energy. You can also try inhaling the energy of your Mantra Ball until it fills your system, like we did in the previous practice.

Most importantly, just play and explore with a sense of wonder. Remember, a mantra is just a tool of thought to anchor the mind. It's not about the specific words but about *how you use the words*. Be creative. You'll get better with practice.

Let's begin.

GUIDED PRACTICE 10

The Mantra Compatibility Test

Time: 10 minutes (but feel free to go longer if you need more time)

STEP 1   Activate the Freedom Trinity to bring yourself to a state of openness and relaxation.

STEP 2   Try each of the eight techniques to test out your mantra. Feel free to reread the techniques while you practice—opening your eyes to read for a moment won't disturb the experience. You're free to combine multiple techniques. The only goal of this practice is to explore your mantra from all angles.

STEP 3   Once you've finished exploring each of the eight techniques, take note of which ones you resonated with most. You'll be using your favorite techniques throughout the rest of the book to build your Daily Meditation Ritual.

Go ahead, practice now. Then read what your fellow workshop participants experienced.

LISA tried repeating the mantra "Salty rocks" in her mind, and then she started to whisper it aloud. Suddenly, she began to hear the sound of the ocean in her mind—the mantra was still present, it just took on a different form of thought. Then she started to feel sad because she missed her father, whom she's been a bit distant from ever since she began awakening to her privilege. They just haven't been seeing eye to eye lately. At first Lisa wanted to change her mantra because it made her feel sad, but then she remembered our discussion about not avoiding challenging emotions. Sadness is a useful emotion that is safe to feel during meditation and often points us toward healing and growth. It was challenging, but it worked. She is going to keep her mantra as is.

AMBER chose the mantra "Love." She immediately started thinking about her daughter, the purest representation of love in her life. Then she started to feel the pulse of her own heartbeat, which brought back the memory of hearing her daughter's heartbeat for the first time when she was pregnant. She saw an image of the word "LOVE" in neon pink lights flashing in her mind, which prompted hundreds of seemingly random renditions of what love could be and what it looks like. She pondered several questions and ideas, like: How can she be more loving to her own mother? How can she reignite the quality of love between her and her husband to be like it was before they had kids? How can she show more love and devotion to God? Amber's mantra brought her into an entire universe of love with the potential for endless exploration. She is going to keep it.

JORDAN picked "Clarity and peace" as his mantra. He was too shy to repeat the mantra aloud, so he whispered it to himself. As soon as he welcomed the mantra into his mind, he thought about the "I have a dream" vision he wrote for his future, but then he started to doubt it. All the uncertainty bubbled up: What job was he going to find? How would he make enough money to live alone? Should he go back to school? What would his major be if he did go back? Was gaining more debt worth it? For the next several minutes, Jordan was overwhelmed with voices in his head asking question after question. Then he remembered he was meditating and returned to his mantra. This time, he decided to leave "clarity" out and just focus on the word "peace." His breath immediately deepened, and he felt more relaxed. After the meditation ended, Jordan was tempted to change his mantra to "Peace," but on the basis of his experience, I suggested he keep the original mantra. The only reason he wanted to remove the word "clarity" was to avoid the challenging questions. When I asked him to describe the experience, he said, "It's interesting, because it's not pleasant, but it's working." Although the word "clarity" raised some unpleasant emotions, it was doing its job and will ultimately lead him to find the answers he's been searching for. Jordan is reluctantly keeping "Clarity and peace" as his mantra for now.

DAVID chose the phrase "Ray of the sun" as his mantra. He started repeating the words silently in his mind and immediately pictured the sun shining on him. He kept seeing rays of sunlight landing on his skin and imagined himself sitting on the beach bathing in that sunlight. It felt great to him, but his experience with the mantra stopped there, and after a few minutes he got bored. He kept trying to force himself to go back to that same image of the beach he had during the first couple of minutes, but it felt flat. The rays of sun made him feel good and comfortable, but overall his experience was one-dimensional. When asked to describe his experience, David said, "I had a few thoughts, but it didn't really take me places. I felt indifferent about it. It was just meh."

David should change his mantra.

HOW TO KNOW IF YOU NEED TO CHANGE YOUR MANTRA

Your first experience with your mantra does not need to be an instantly life-changing experience—remember, this is a first date. You should feel intrigued enough, however, to want to take your mantra on a second date. A good first date should leave you with the sense that there's more to explore, even if you might be unsure or nervous about it.

The only feeling that warrants changing a mantra is if you feel totally blank—an experience of disinterest and boredom. In simple terms, if your first experience with your mantra makes you go, "Blah" or "Meh," like it did for David, you have permission to change it right away.

Be careful, because sometimes fear can trick you into changing your mantra prematurely. Remember, feeling an "undesirable" emotion does *not* warrant an immediate mantra change. Many of us who have grown up with trauma will have unresolved wounds that need to be tended to. Your meditation practice will (and should) bring those wounds to the surface. Do not run from them. The transformation you are looking for is inside of all that pain. Just because it doesn't feel good doesn't mean it's not working.

In the same regard, I don't want you to torture yourself with a consistently painful mantra. Unresolved wounds will surface, but they should not be the main dish of your entire meditation practice. If your mantra *always* makes you feel heavy and dark, day after day, with no light at the end of the tunnel, you have permission to change it.

If you've decided to change your mantra, here's what you should do right now before continuing with the book:

OPTION 1 Try slightly refining your mantra. Manipulate the words a bit, add a new word, or change the order of the words to see how it alters the flavor.

OPTION 2 Go back to Guided Practice 9 and take yourself through the Mantra Ball practice again to source a brand-new mantra. Be open to whatever arises.

Either way, don't judge yourself if you need change your mantra. Many students do.

If you go through the process more than three times and still do not land on a mantra you like, there is a high likelihood that you are experiencing fear and resistance to this practice. Here's what I suggest: pick a mantra and stick with it for the rest of this book. Indecisiveness is often a disguised form of fear trying to stop you from up-leveling your life. Don't let it stop you. Just pick one and continue learning. You can always change it later.

Your workshop buddy **DAVID** had a flat experience with his mantra, so he changed it. When he went back through the Mantra Ball practice, he saw rays of sun again, but this time he said his mantra in Spanish, since it's his native language. He changed it to *"Soy el sol brillante,"* which directly translates to "I am the brilliant sun," but that doesn't do it any justice—we don't have a word quite like *brillante* in English. It's a combination of brilliant, shiny, radiant, and sparkling—but it has a majestic feeling to it that invokes a sense of awe and wonder, like the inner spark you get when you see the perfect sunset or hear a motivational speech that blows you away. The Spanish version had so much more life and texture for David that as soon as he changed it, the entire experienced deepened for him. When he said the words *"Soy el sol brillante,"* David's mantra transformed into an image of the sun above his head; he could feel the heat and the warmth of the sun on his skin. The golden light entered his body and cleansed him of the resistance and pain he felt from the constant pressure of trying to become a successful artist. It also energized him and inspired a sudden fit of gratitude. He couldn't stop grinning. Just before the timer rang, David imagined actually being on the sun, all of his toxic habits and thoughts burning away in the fire of transformation.

With just a slight alteration, David's mantra became perfect for him.

If you're all set with *your* mantra, let's continue.

MANTRAS BELIEVE IN MONOGAMY

It's time to move on to the next phase of the relationship: monogamy. Don't worry, you'll be able to open the relationship later, but to start, your mantra requires commitment. I've spent quite a bit of time studying the qualities of healthy open relationships, and believe it or not, similar rules apply to meditation. If you ask anyone who has been in a successful open relationship, they will tell you that

IF YOU GO THROUGH
A PHASE OF BOREDOM
OR TENSION, TRY

MOVING
CLOSER

TO YOUR MANTRA
INSTEAD OF MOVING
AWAY FROM IT.

the most important element is building a strong foundation of trust with your primary partner. If you open the relationship prematurely—because you're bored, because you're chasing the thrill, because you have trouble committing—it will all fall apart. The same is true with your mantra.

You *must* build a deep level of intimacy with your mantra first. You can learn to be a polyamorous meditator after the relationship matures.

I tell most of my students to stick with their mantra for a minimum of forty days to give it time to excavate their minds and make connections. For example, you may have a particular thought during one week of your meditation and then three weeks later have another seemingly random thought. Time will pass, and you'll gain some life experience, and then suddenly your mantra will connect those two seemingly random thoughts, opening a new pathway for your growth. This cannot happen without time and consistency.

Although forty days is my suggested minimum, the deeper level of practice comes when you commit to one mantra until your soul knows it's time to move on.

When I started using "Complete authenticity" as my mantra, I was living a life that desperately needed changing. I was successful, but I was not loving my life. I felt like something was missing. I knew that I was not expressing my full power, but I didn't know how to fix it. "Complete authenticity" healed me from the inside out. At the beginning, my mantra was infusing authenticity into my professional life and giving me the courage to make big changes in my career. Then, a few months later, it evolved to eradicate the inauthentic relationships that were stunting my growth. There were weeks when I sang my mantra aloud, whispered it, and dissected each syllable to see what else was inside. On days when I was overwhelmed and stressed, the sound "aaahhhhhhh" in "authenticity" helped me exhale and relax. The word "come" within "complete" helped me manifest my music career, as if I was enchanting my album to reveal itself to me. There's a syllable in "Complete authenticity" that even managed to liberate my sexual energy—but the details of that transformation are for another type of book.

By committing to your mantra, you give it time to mature. I stuck with my mantra for two full years before I changed it. Did it get boring sometimes? Yes. Did I think about ditching it for a new mantra every once in a while? Yes. Did

I get upset with it for not fulfilling all my lofty expecations? Absolutely. This is where commitment comes in. If you go through a phase of boredom or tension, try moving closer to your mantra instead of turning away from it. Explore the mantra more intimately—dissect and indulge in it. Usually a challenging phase is just a cue that a new pathway is opening. If you abandon your mantra too early, you will only scratch the surface of its power and never experience the deep levels of transformational growth it has to offer.

When your mantra is done doing its work on you, you will know. You will feel it lose its power. Allow your mantra to be a constant in your life. Through the good times and the bad, through sickness and in health, it will be there for you with open arms, always welcoming you home to yourself.

Essential Points from This Chapter

- *Mantra* means "tool of thought."

- Your mantra can be any word or combination of words. Don't judge it!

- There are eight ways to try out your mantra: silently, aloud, quietly, slowly, rapidly, in rhythm with your breath, using the 6S Thought Spectrum, or using your Mantra Ball.

- If your mantra makes you go, "Meh," you should change it.

- If your mantra feels consistently heavy and dark, you should change it.

- Don't change your mantra in avoidance of difficult emotions. Just because it doesn't feel good doesn't mean it's not working.

- If you get bored with your mantra, move closer to it instead of turning away.

CHAPTER

7

We Practice Presence

If you've studied other forms of meditation, you may have been told to ignore or push down your emotions. But your emotions are like the herbs and spices of meditation: without them, the practice is watered down, bland, and boring.

In Freedom Meditation, we practice being present with every feeling, sensation, and emotion as it arises spontaneously. Sometimes you will feel restless, anxious, and overwhelmed. Other times you will feel joyous, relaxed, and peaceful. Welcome all of it. That's when the magic happens.

I learned this lesson when I was eighteen years old and got to inverview Christina Aguilera at the taping of a special broadcast for her album premiere. It was a total emotional roller coaster. You have to understand, I was an Xtina superfan. I had every magazine cover scotch-taped to my bedroom wall when I was a kid, went to every concert (multiple times), and know every growl, riff, run, and live performance in her catalog by heart. When I arrived on set, there were only about a hundred people in the audience. We were in a beautifully designed, small, smoky room with hundreds of lights, big television cameras, and security guards everywhere—I had never seen anything like it. At that point, I didn't know I would be interviewing her yet; I was just excited to be breathing the same air as Christina freakin' Aguilera. The joy was beaming off of me. And even though I knew I looked a little ridiculous—frolicking around the theater and smiling at everyone in sight—I just couldn't help myself. Then, out of the blue, a man with a walkie-talkie came up to me and said, "Hey, young man, do you want to interview Christina?" I was in shock. "What?!" I said. I must've been hallucinating. He repeated, "Look, kid, we don't have a lot of time, but we're looking for audience

YOU CAN BE RESTFUL OR RESTLESS, ANXIOUS OR EXCITED, SAD OR HAPPY, AND STILL BE MEDITATING THE ENTIRE TIME.

members to interview Christina on the show, and we think you'd be a perfect fit. If you want to do it, come with me." I jumped up so quickly you would've thought my chair had caught on fire. Then I followed that man all the way to the stage, where he sat me front and center. That's where she was going to be—just seven feet away from me. I was overwhelmed with anticipation. Here I was, this small-town boy who had just moved to Los Angeles for college, about to interview my idol on camera. Baby, you couldn't tell me nothin'! As I waited over the course of the next three hours, I oscillated somewhere between a complete meltdown and total rapture. Every emotion possible ran through my system—anxiety, fear, excitement, joy, awe, and straight-up terror. The emotions were so strong, I couldn't control them or push them down no matter how hard I tried. So when the moment finally came and I stood up on the stage to interview her, my emotions went wild. I started crying my eyes out. So much so that the producers asked me to do the interview three different times in order for them to get a good enough take to use on air. Christina called me "cutie," and we giggled together between takes for a solid twenty minutes. So not only did I get to interview my idol *once*, but I did it *three times* and got to laugh and hang out with her on stage—a moment that never would've happened had I pushed down my emotions.

When we push down our emotions, force too much control over our minds, or make a goal out of everything, we lose the opportunity to be with *what is*—the natural, spontaneous, authentic pulse of life.

In this chapter, I am going to guide you through understanding how to welcome your emotions (even the challenging ones), how to anchor your mind when it's going crazy, and how to use meditation as a supplement to your healing.

RESTFULNESS TO RESTLESSNESS

This is important. The diagram below illustrates the organic fluctuations between restfulness and restlessness in the brain. This is what happens in your mind when you meditate.

Most people think meditation is the cycle of restfulness and restlessness itself, when in fact meditation is the box that surrounds the entire cycle (as illustrated in the diagram). It's totally common and natural for you to alternate between

feelings of restfulness and restlessness throughout your practice—we all do. You might even feel restless the entire time or oscillate between the two within a matter of seconds. You can be restful or restless, anxious or excited, sad or happy, *and still be meditating the entire time*. This is normal, even for people who have been meditating for many years.

Think of it like going to the gym. During a workout, it's normal to have moments of extreme physical exertion followed by moments of rest. The moments of rest are just as valuable as the physically demanding moments. You would never say that you "aren't working out" just because you decided to rest for a few minutes in between sets. A successful workout requires the fluctuations between effort and rest. Meditation is exactly the same. So when you experience a moment of restfulness during your practice, enjoy it, bask in it, but do not try to grip it—the anticipation of it leaving only activates more restlessness. The path to enjoying meditation requires cycling through periods of restfulness and restlessness without any force or restraint.

DON'T ALWAYS EXPECT TO FEEL THE BENEFITS OF MEDITATION *DURING* YOUR PRACTICE

If you ask most meditators, they will tell you that they often feel the positive benefits of meditation *after* they're done meditating, not during their practice. Going to the gym is not typically relaxing, but when you're done exercising, you always feel a sense of aliveness that lasts throughout the day. Cleaning your house feels like work, but once you finish, you can enjoy the comfort of your uncluttered space. These actual processes themselves are not typically relaxing, but when the work is complete you are able to enjoy the fruits of your labor as you engage with your life. Meditation works the same way. Put in the work, and you'll move through your life with a greater sense of alignment and a clearer mind.

WHEN YOU REALIZE YOU'RE LOST IN THOUGHT, PIVOT TO YOUR MANTRA WITHOUT JUDGMENT OR FORCE.

EVERYTHING THAT ARISES IN THE PRESENCE OF YOUR MANTRA IS TO BE CONSIDERED VALUABLE AND PURPOSEFUL, EVEN IF YOU DON'T UNDERSTAND IT.

Here's the big takeaway: You're not just meditating when you're relaxed; you're meditating for as long as the timer is set for your practice. And everything that happens within that time is fair game so long as your mantra is present.

HOW TO USE YOUR MANTRA TO ANCHOR YOUR MIND (IT'S EASY!)

Remember what we discussed in chapter 1 about myths: what stops most people from meditating is believing they're supposed to get their mind to to stop thinking. This is not true, possible, or natural. The goal of meditation is *not* to get the mind to stop thinking. Instead, you must anchor your thoughts to work *for you* rather than against you.

Your mantra is your anchor.

Using your mantra as an anchor is simple: whenever thoughts begin to arise during meditation, simply welcome yourself back to your mantra just as easily as you drifted away from it. When you realize you're lost in thought, pivot to your mantra without judgment or force—think of it as a gentle reminder to return to home base.

Let's practice.

The goal of the next guided practice is to notice the cycles of restfulness and restlessness that are coming up for you today and to gain some experience using your mantra as a tool to anchor your mind amid that cycle. Learning this technique is a vital part of meditation, but it will take some practice. Be patient with yourself. Your experience will differ every time you meditate, so don't get attached to a specific feeling. Allow every thought, feeling, sensation, and emotion to arise and use your mantra as a tool to welcome yourself back as often as needed. There is no minimum or maximum number of times that you should be using your mantra, and it should never be a goal to use your mantra less frequently. Use it as freely and as often as you need to.

GUIDED PRACTICE 11

How to Get Centered When Your Mind Is Going Crazy

Time: 5 minutes

STEP 1   Initiate the Freedom Trinity by sitting comfortably, engaging your eyes, taking some deep breaths, and going inward.

STEP 2   Bring your mantra into your mind. Remember, you can use any technique that works for you—bringing it to mind silently, aloud, quietly, slowly, rapidly, in rhythm with your breath, using the 6S Thought Spectrum, or using your Mantra Ball.

STEP 3   Practice anchoring your mind with your mantra amid the cycles of restfulness and restlessness. When you realize you've drifted far away from your mantra, welcome yourself back just as easily as you drifted away from it.

I already know what you're thinking . . . **How do you know you're not just daydreaming instead of meditating?**

Know this: your mind is never wandering during meditation—it's rehearsing for your life.

If you've ever played a sport or performed an art form of any kind, you understand the importance of rehearsal. When we rehearse, we build our confidence, we practice our skill, and we prepare ourselves for the moments that matter most. Think about how powerful it is, then, if your mind is practicing and rehearsing for the game of life in meditation.

During meditation, your brain is going through a mental rehearsal so that when a situation arises, your mind has already mapped out all the good, bad, and maybe even crazy scenarios that could potentially play out. This way, when you face the situation in your real life, your brain has already processed and made the necessary connections to allow you to make the best decision.

The presence of a mantra is what turns daydreaming into purpose-driven meditation. Everything that arises in the presence of your mantra is to be considered valuable and purposeful, even if you don't understand it. So next time you're meditating, instead of labeling your thoughts as "daydreaming," just think of them as a mental rehearsal. This will change everything for you.

TURN TOWARD YOUR PAIN: HEALING YOUR WOUNDS WITH MEDITATION

The unique essence of your mantra is going to attract the thoughts, memories, and emotions that need to be healed by its energy, so it's important that you don't run away from your restless thoughts, pain, anger, sadness, or any emotion you've labeled as "bad." I repeat: *do not run away from difficult emotions*. It's been proven that suppressing your feelings leads to all kinds of bad stuff. For example, pushing down your "negative" emotions also inhibits your ability to express *positive* emotions—so the more you suppress, the less happiness you'll experience in the long run. It also raises your heart rate, impairs your memory, and causes you to be less liked by your friends because they can

IT'S OKAY TO BE ANGRY, IT'S OKAY TO BE UPSET, IT'S OKAY TO BE IN A SHITTY MOOD— YOU DON'T ALWAYS NEED TO FIX IT.

sense your lack of vulnerability (even when you think you're faking it).[1] The key is acceptance.

Writing about this reminds me of the summer of 2017. My gosh . . . that was tough. I dealt with a breakup, the biggest show on my tour was suddenly canceled (which left me broke AF), and I spiraled into my first-ever encounter with depression. How was it that I, Justin Michael Williams—the guy who everyone expected to be so motivating and inspiring—could feel so heavy and dark? I felt totally alone and confused, like I was lost at sea. I was lethargic; I didn't want to do anything; and, to top it off, I was gaining weight and losing the sculpted body I had worked so hard for. I wanted to reach out for help, but I didn't feel like I could talk to anyone, because even my closest friends and family members expected me to be a beacon of positivity and happiness.

Besides therapy, the only place I could go for healing was my meditation practice. During this time, my practice was challenging. It intensified the pain, but I found that meditating made my therapy sessions more effective. Plus I knew from my years of study that meditation is proven to help with depression, so I committed to sitting for fifteen minutes every day.[2] Some days I would cry, I'd be upset, I'd be anxious, I'd be mad, or I'd beat myself up for not being more successful—I felt every emotion other than happy and relaxed. Other days it would get so intense that I would skip my practice altogether. But during this process, even if it would take me a few days or a week, I always found a lifeline guiding me toward the next stage of my healing. I wanted so badly for a huge revelation to pull me completely out of my depression. I wanted to rush the process. I wanted to hear the voice of God shouting to me with immediate answers to all of my questions. But sometimes the lifeline you need is not a big "aha!" moment. Sometimes it's just a whisper that says, "Oh, you need to call that person." And then that seemingly random phone call leads to another step, and another step, and another. And soon, instead of drowning, you're on the shore.

It doesn't matter how much you meditate, how spiritual you are, or how good of a person you are: we all experience difficult emotions from time to time. And if the trauma is severe or you're in a serious bout of depression, don't be afraid to seek professional support—sometimes meditation isn't enough, and asking for professional help doesn't make you weak. Lean into your pain. I know it's not easy, my love, but do not avoid it. The goal of meditation is *not* to elevate your mood so that you never have to feel discomfort. That is called "spiritual bypassing," which is just as dismissive as saying #AllLivesMatter. In order to heal, we must attend to the places within our own selves that are broken, wounded, and hurt. It's okay to be angry, it's okay to be upset, it's okay to be in a shitty mood—you don't always need to fix it. Sometimes you just need to get fucking mad about something! If the only emotions you are comfortable expressing are peace and love, you risk living a life of complacent mediocrity just so you don't ruffle any feathers.

In the safe embrace of your meditation practice, you can explore the *full spectrum* of your healthy emotions, which is essential to both your mental and your physical health.[3] I know it can feel messy and confronting, but trust me: the life waiting for you on the other side of all that pain is more vibrant than you could ever imagine. When we allow our pain to surface during meditation, we build an intimate relationship with it and transform our trauma into empowerment. And this is not just some woo-woo self-help stuff. Science has proven that mindfulness meditation helps you become more resilient in the face of challenges.[4] The more you meditate, the less severe your reactions will be when the hard stuff happens, and the more likely you'll be able to experience growth.

The magic is in the mess. Get in there.

THE MAGIC IS IN THE MESS.

IT'S NOT ALWAYS THAT DEEP

Although I'm placing a huge emphasis on your thoughts and emotions, please remember that *you are not your thoughts* and *everything doesn't mean something*. Every thought will not offer a life-changing epiphany—some thoughts just need to be released. The more junk you release, the fewer unresolved wounds take up space in your mind, and the clearer you'll be able to think. This is why people who meditate often feel a greater sense of life satisfaction than people who don't.

How all of your thoughts are related to the bigger picture of your life is not for you to worry about. Let your mantra be the bait that lures your thoughts with its natural essence. When you need to know something, you will know. And you will get better at knowing as your practice sharpens your intuition over time. We will discuss strengthening your intuition a little later in the book.

Now it's time to experiment with all the new information you've learned. Take a moment to read what your fellow workshop participants experienced, paying extra close attention to how they used their mantras, their forms of thought, as well as the correlation between their mantra choices and thought patterns. This will help you understand how it works in your own mind. See if you can spot their moments of mental rehearsal, restfulness, and restlessness. Then we will do a short practice together so you can feel how these concepts work for you.

DAVID used the words of his mantra *"Soy el sol brillante"* only once, at the very beginning of his practice; then the words immediately morphed into feelings and images. He could feel the warmth of the sun on his body and imagine the sunlight burning away all his toxic habits. Feelings of hope and peace overtook him for about ninety seconds, but then his anxiety started to surface: he was stressed about paying rent this month because he spent too much money on Beyoncé concert tickets; he went on three different auditions this week but had not gotten a callback for any of the roles yet; plus he needed to figure out how he was going to pay someone to build his new website. Then he randomly started thinking about his friend's birthday party coming up at a local bar and how he should avoid spending money on drinks to save for rent. "But what the hell," he thought. "I've been working so hard, I deserve a few drinks." And then he remembered he was meditating and brought back the image of the sun, but this time he became the sun, with radiant golden light beaming out of his chest in all directions.

The energy of the sun is illuminating so much about David's internal world. It is revealing the places he needs to focus, what he needs to heal, and the habits he needs to release so that he can stop falling into the same toxic cycles over and over. Although this may take David some time to realize, the practice is working on him.

LISA started her practice with her eyes open, repeating the mantra "Salty rocks" aloud and very slowly. Soon she started hearing the sound of the ocean, and she felt relaxed. But that lasted only for about twenty seconds, because she immediately realized how privileged she was to be a young girl watching her dad surf while so many other children in the world barely had enough food to eat, let alone the opportunity to enjoy the beach. It made her want to cry, but the image of tears reminded her of the ocean again, which brought her back to her mantra, "Salty rocks, salty rocks, salty rocks," which she repeated this time in a whisper. She began to see the waves of the ocean crashing into her own heart, filling her with a sense of connection to all things. She sat in this feeling of expanding peace for several minutes, and for the first time in a while she felt comfortable enough to close her eyes. Once she became conscious of how long she had been peaceful, she was surprised and then tried to grip onto it, which sent her back into a restless state. She spent the final moments of her meditation trying to recreate that peaceful scene with the waves crashing into her heart, but it didn't feel the same, so she got annoyed and felt like she was doing it wrong.

Did you notice how Lisa's practice was going perfectly until she started gripping onto the feeling of peace? Learning to rest in the embrace of peacefulness without anticipating it fleeing takes some practice, but it's worth it. Over time, meditation will expand your capacity to experience joy.

JORDAN has a family gathering coming up later this week, so he's been extra-anxious about everyone asking him the dreaded question "What are you doing with your life?" As soon as his meditation started, the anxiety got worse. "Clarity and peace, clarity and peace, clarity and peace"—he repeated the mantra in his mind like a drill sergeant, trying to make the anxiety go away. For the next few moments, he sat annoyed, wondering if meditation was the right thing for him.

Jordan is running from his emotions and attempting to use his mantra to distract him from the anxiety that is so desperately trying to get his attention. He's expending so much energy pushing down his feelings that he can't see the open field of possibility in front of him. What is his anxiety trying to reveal to him? If only he would allow himself to feel the emotion instead of pushing it down, he would find the lifeline.

AMBER used the Mantra Ball technique. She thought of the word "Love" and then saw a transparent, pastel-pink ball of energy with silver shimmery glitter inside of it. She imagined herself sitting in front of this ball as it expanded until it engulfed her entire body. Inside this ball, she felt an unusual yet beautiful sense of stillness. There was no sound. No one needed her. And no kids were calling for help. She was alone and felt like everyone and everything was taken care of. Then she thought about her phone and got nervous because she had turned it on silent for her meditation. What if her daughter's school called? What if there was an emergency? This made her anxious, and she wanted to jump out of the practice early to check her phone. She would never forgive herself if something happened to her daughter and she missed the call. The war between self-care and selfishness raged in Amber's mind. Her heart started to race as she imagined something bad happening to her daughter. And then she remembered to come back to her mantra, so she tried repeating the word "Love" over and over aloud, but this made her more anxious. She sat for a few more minutes and then grabbed her phone to check for a missed call. There were none.

Amber's meditation allowed her to rehearse the experience of putting herself first. It gave her a visceral demonstration of how she equates self-care with being selfish. She is learning, albeit slowly, how to love herself while still caring for her family at the same time. Rehearsing her anxiety response in a meditative state will teach Amber how to manage her stress in real life so that she can start to make choices from a place of love rather than fear.

Now it's your turn. Let's do a quick practice to give you an intimate experience with your own thoughts.

GUIDED PRACTICE 12

Turn Your Mess into Magic

Time: 5 minutes

STEP 1   As usual, start with the Freedom Trinity.

STEP 2   Use your favorite techniques to welcome your mantra into your mind.

STEP 3   Allow every thought to arise naturally as you oscillate between restfulness and restlessness, using your mantra to anchor your mind when you drift too far away.

STEP 4   When you're done meditating, see if you can draw any connections between your mantra and your thoughts. What were you rehearsing for? Were there any seemingly random thoughts? What was the overall theme of this particular meditation?

It's okay if you don't remember everything—that's not the point. Your experience will evolve and change with every practice. You'll get better at making connections as you learn more.

Essential Points from This Chapter

- When thoughts arise, welcome yourself back to your mantra just as easily as you drifted away from it.

- It is natural for you to fluctuate between feelings of restfulness and restlessness throughout your practice. Allow it.

- Don't expect to feel the benefits of meditation during your practice— sometimes it feels like work.

- It's okay if your mind wanders during meditation—it is rehearsing for your life.

- Your mantra will attract the thoughts that need to be healed by its energy

- Don't run away from difficult emotions during meditation. The magic is in the mess.

- Not every thought will offer a life-changing epiphany; some thoughts just need to be released.

CHAPTER

8

we get

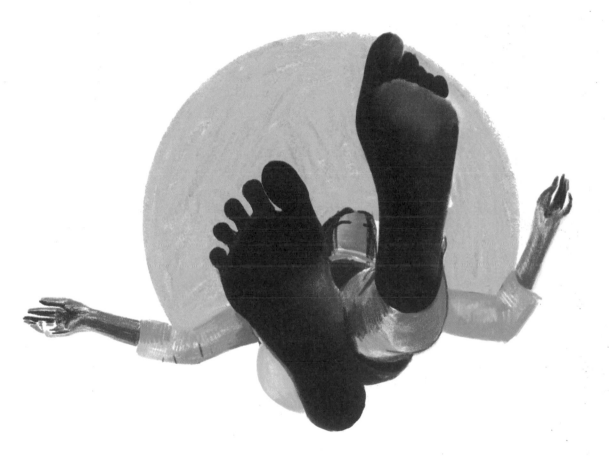

physical

remember the first time I ever went hiking. I was twenty-three, and my boyfriend at the time had been trying to drag me on a hike for months, but I always scoffed at the idea and told him, "Black people don't hike" (toxic belief, anyone?). But one day, after making every excuse in the book ("I have asthma," "I don't like bugs," "I'm too hot"), I finally agreed to go on a hike for his birthday. We drove along the ocean up the Pacific Coast Highway, all the way to the trailhead of the most beautiful hike in the Santa Monica Mountains. It's called Paseo Miramar and is about a ninety-minute round-trip hike with stunning panoramic views of the Pacific Ocean.

Guess how long I lasted?

Fifteen minutes.

I thought I was in shape. I thought I was athletic. Hell, I had been doing yoga, Pilates, and weight lifting for years, but after just a few minutes on that trail, I damn near had to call a helicopter to come rescue us (and it wasn't even that hard of a trail!).

It doesn't matter how much you train or how in shape you think you are: when you try a new type of movement, muscles get activated that you didn't even know existed. The same thing happens when you add physical movement to your meditation practice. Mental pathways get activated that you didn't even know existed. Physical movement is an essential and delicious ingredient to add to your meditation recipe.

MOVEMENT: THE NATURAL RHYTHM OF MEDITATION

Movement can enhance your meditation practice. In fact, it is essential for most people. Yet many meditation styles ignore the body completely. What

LLNESS

IS OVERRATED.

I know to be true is that your physical body is just as important a part of your practice as your mind—the health of your body is scientifically proven to impact your mental health. It has become widely known that even light physical movement has the power to relieve stress, boost your overall mood, alleviate anxiety, cure insomnia, slow the aging process, and treat depression as effectively as antidepressant medication. When you read that list, you might notice that physical movement and seated meditation actually share many of the same benefits, so imagine how much more powerful it is when you combine the two.

Stillness is overrated. Nothing in the universe is still. Not your body, not your mind, and not this planet. So why would we ever expect to find complete stillness in meditation? It's unnatural and unnecessary.

I want to be clear here: I'm not suggesting that you *force* movement into your practice or that your meditation become a dance routine. All I want is for you to give yourself permission to move *when and if it feels natural to you*. You might allow your body to gently sway from side to side, pulsing with the rhythm of your breath for your entire practice. Or you might sit completely still for a few minutes and then pulse for a few and return to stillness again. In Freedom Meditation, we are breaking free from the bondage of rigidy and confinement. I encourage you to welcome movement to your practice. It will help you connect to the natural rhythm of your life.

The next guided practice is called Pulse. The goal is simple: to experience movement during meditation. As your practice develops, you can explore more dramatic movements, like walking or even dancing, but for now, I want you to start by sitting, because too much movement can turn into a convenient distraction when you're first getting started.

GUIDED PRACTICE 13

Pulse: For Meditators Who Hate Sitting Still

Time: 5 minutes

STEP 1   As usual, use the Freedom Trinity to get started.

STEP 2   Welcome your mantra to your practice.

STEP 3   Start to deepen your breath. Notice how on the inhales, your body gets larger and takes up more space, and on the exhales, your body contracts and gets just a little smaller.

STEP 4   Now exaggerate that. As you inhale and exhale, allow your body to expand and contract. Let it sway and pulse, forward and backward and from side to side, with the rhythm of your breath.

STEP 5   Exaggerate your movements *even more*. Start to move your arms. Allow your torso to sway and rock. Try both dramatic and subtle movements to see how they shift your experience.

STEP 6   Move *even more*. Be spontaneous. Allow your body and arms to sway, pulse, and move as if you are doing a slow seated dance through water with your breath as the soundtrack. Don't think about it too much—there's no right or wrong way to do this. Give yourself permission to look like a complete fool for a minute.

STEP 7   When your timer rings, come back to center, sit up tall, and open your eyes.

Take a moment to pause and reflect. How was this experience for you? Be honest.

If you loved it, onward!

If not, you aren't alone.

Movement has become one of my favorite ingredients of the Freedom Meditation recipe, but it wasn't always that way. I used to judge myself, worry about looking silly, and be totally afraid to express emotion with my body. Movement can be triggering for many of us. If that's the case for you, it's okay. Welcome whatever emotions arise. You're opening a new pathway, like I did on my first hike. As you get more seasoned in your meditation practice, you can try adding movement again if you want. Up to you!

WE ARE ALL ENERGY HEALERS

Most people have that one person in their family who seems to have a slight touch of magic. In my family, that person was my Baca. She always knew if someone was pregnant, even before they announced it; she predicted the sex of everyone's babies with 100 percent accuracy; and she had a telepathic way of knowing when I needed help, even though I lived hundreds of miles away. But her greatest gift was something I came to know as "Hot Hands." Anytime someone in our family was sick, hurt, or struggling, my Baca would invite them to lay down on the carpet in her *special* living room (the room every black grandma had back in the day where the furniture would usually be covered in plastic). Once they got down on the floor, my Baca would rub her hands together to heat them up, say a prayer, and then place her warm hands on the spot that needed healing. Sometimes her hands would get so hot that her touch would burn, but she never budged. She would just sit in a constant state of prayer and allow her hands to be a conduit of healing energy.

One of my first and most vivid memories of watching her heal was when I was about eight years old. I woke up in the middle of the night to get some water. As I tiptoed into the kitchen, I heard a noise in the special living room, which I thought was weird because no one was ever allowed to go into that room. I peeked around the corner and saw my dad lying facedown on the floor, shirtless, with a towel underneath him. My Baca was leaning over him with her eyes closed and her hands on my dad's lower back. Drops of sweat were dripping from his entire body, soaking through the towel and seeping onto the floor. When I first saw this, I didn't know what was happening; I was actually scared because I could feel the intensity of the moment. The energy was thick. I watched for a few seconds but then scurried back to my room before anyone knew I was there. The following week, I learned that my dad was scheduled to have surgery on his lower back. When he arrived at the pre-op appointment, the doctors called the entire staff into the room. They couldn't believe what they saw. They came out to the waiting room and told us that they'd never seen anything like it, but it "appeared" as though my father had scar tissue in his lower back, as if he'd already undergone the surgery—but he hadn't.

My Baca grinned and said, "I thought so. Let's get going. I'm hungry." She was totally unfazed by the event, as if this supernatural healing was normal. The doctors called off the surgery, and in that moment I knew, with certainty, that we have access to a universal healing energy that is more powerful than we can even fathom.

It was not until my late teens that I finally had the guts to share that story with my Baca. I was too afraid to tell her that I was eavesdropping in the middle of the night. She laughed and said, "Well, Lawd, if you woulda told me sooner, I would've let you know you have the same power too, baby."

And then she taught me Hot Hands.

Hot Hands is a way that you can heal and soothe your physical body with the power of your mantra.

It's really simple, and the feeling is subtle. Let's try it.

Hot Hands

Time: 3 minutes

STEP 1   Initiate the Freedom Trinity.

STEP 2   Invite your mantra forward using your favorite techniques.

STEP 3   Rub your palms together vigorously for about 60 seconds to build some heat in your hands.

STEP 4   After you stop rubbing, immediately place your palms over your eyes *without touching your face at all*. Get as close as you can without touching.

STEP 5   Imagine the energy of your mantra radiating from your hands and bathing your eyes, face, and mind. You may actually feel physical heat, or you might just imagine rays of light (akin to the energy from your Mantra Ball) glowing from your hands.

STEP 6   Rub your hands together again, place your hands near a different area of the body, and repeat step 5 on this new part of your body. You can repeat this as many times as you'd like.

Note: Remember, don't actually touch your body with your hands—keep them a few centimeters away.

AMBER, our busy mom, is in desperate need of some self-care, so she placed her Hot Hands over her chest to send the energy of love straight into her heart center. She didn't really feel much heat, but she could imagine the pink, shimmery energy infiltrating her heart.

DAVID and JORDAN are both dealing with anxiety, so they placed their hands near their foreheads to ease their minds.

LISA used Hot Hands on the front and back of her throat, inspiring her to speak her truth. She wants to get more comfortable speaking up about issues like activism and privilege.

I use this practice often, especially if I'm feeling sick or if I have aches and pains that I suspect are coming from stress and anxiety.

Remember, this is a subtle practice. And, just like my dad, you may not instantaneously notice or feel the benefits in an obvious way. But with trust, faith, and a little practice, the healing power of Hot Hands will be proven to you.

Essential Points from This Chapter

- You don't have to sit completely still during meditation. Allow your body to pulse and move.

- Movements during meditation should feel spontaneous and natural, never forced.

- Use Hot Hands to infuse the energy of your mantra into your physical body.

- When you're practicing Hot Hands, remember to keep your hands a few centimeters away from the spot you're healing.

CHAPTER

9

we want answers

Cooking with my Baca was about more than just food. It was a time to be together and talk about some of life's most challenging questions—she was the one person I could call upon anytime I needed advice or support—and nothing was off-limits. It didn't matter if I was asking about dating, sex, love, school, work, friends, or food, Baca was always there to support me with her wisdom. And after instilling me with her sage advice, she would often say, "You already got all the answers you need inside you, baby. I'm just here to remind you when you forget." Receiving wisdom was one of the best things about cooking with my Baca, and it's also one of my favorite ingredients in our Freedom Meditation recipe.

HOW TO GET THE ANSWERS
YOU'VE BEEN SEARCHING FOR

Meditation can help you make better decisions and answer questions in moments of uncertainty.[1] But the process of gaining wisdom and receiving answers to life's tough questions does not usually happen in the way you would think.

If you're expecting to hear a mystical voice thundering with revolutionary answers to every question within ten minutes of meditating, you're in for a disappointment. It just doesn't work that way. You will rarely get the answers you are looking for during the same session in which you ask the questions. That might happen every once in a while, but more frequently you'll experience what I call a *feedback delay*. Feedback delay requires you to go out onto the stage of your life to play, explore, and gain some experience before you're ready to hear the answers you've been searching for.

I have about a million examples of this, but one of my favorites is the time when I was searching for the title of my debut album of music. I meditated every day for weeks and created lists of about a hundred possible titles, but none of them felt quite right. Then one day I got a text message from my friend Sianna Sherman. I had just sent her a few preview images from a photo shoot I did for my first single. I was nervous about the new photos because they were pretty risqué (I was naked, covered in paint), and up until that point the public had only ever seen me as a preppy professional marketing dude, so I wanted to get Sianna's opinion. This was her response: "These are nuts! I'm wild for them. I've never seen you this way! Total metamorphosis."

And just like that, my album title, *Metamorphosis*, was born—from one tiny and seemingly insignificant word in a text message. But because I had tuned my system and activated my RAS so diligently during my daily meditation practice, I was able to notice the answer the moment it was revealed.

Your life will always give you the answers you need. Think of meditation as tuning yourself to hear the answers as they unfold around you. Your practice will clear out all the junk that has been blocking you from hearing that answer in the first place. Then, even if you are in a bar eavesdropping on the person's conversation next to you, or having a random DM conversation with a friend, or looking at billboards on the highway, or watching television, or doing any other seemingly mundane day-to-day activity, your mind will be clear enough to receive the message when it's ready to be revealed.

WHAT IF I DO HEAR THE VOICE OF GOD?

In those sacred moments when you do hear the voice of God, the universe, or your Higher Power: LISTEN AND TAKE ACTION. You don't need a book to tell you that.

DON'T ASK THE UNIVERSE DUMB QUESTIONS

I hate when people say, "There's no such thing as a dumb question." There are many dumb questions. And most of us go through life asking them. The Bible says, "Ask and you shall receive," so if you're going to spend time asking questions and searching for answers during your meditations, you better stop asking low-quality questions. Low-quality questions lead to low-quality answers. High-quality questions invite possibility, learning, growth, and new ideas.

Pro tip: High-quality questions usually begin with "How . . . ?"

Here are some examples of low-quality (LQ) and high-quality (HQ) questions from your fellow workshop participants.

AMBER

LQ: Why is it so hard for me to lose these last ten pounds?
HQ: How can I lose ten pounds in a way that will be fun and exciting to me?

LISA

LQ: Why is there so much injustice and hatred in the world?
HQ: How can I be of service? How can I use my privilege to help others during this very important moment in our history?

DAVID

LQ: Why am I not getting booked when I go to auditions?
HQ: How can I improve my skills as an actor?

JORDAN

LQ: Why can't I find a job? Why am I always so unmotivated?
HQ: How can I use this opportunity of living at home to have fun and explore things that excite me?

HIGH-QUALITY QUESTIONS REQUIRE YOU TO TAKE RESPONSIBILITY FOR YOUR LIFE.

High-quality questions require you to take responsibility for your life. Low-quality questions just give you more excuses.

HOW TO SOURCE CREATIVE IDEAS FROM MEDITATION

If you're a creative person like me, it's likely that you'll get an overwhelming number of ideas running through your mind during meditation, and all of them are going to seem like great ideas, and you are going to want to stop meditating to write them all down. Don't.

Never try to remember ideas that arise during meditation.

If you effortlessly remember an idea after your meditation is over, pay attention to it. If you finish meditating and an idea is totally gone, forget about it—the mind was just cleaning house.

I know it can be tempting to interrupt your meditation to write things down, but trust that if an idea is meant to manifest in the physical plane, you will remember it no matter what. Some ideas come just to be a catalyst for the *real* idea, so if you interrupt your meditations to write everything down, you risk stopping the idea-formation process prematurely, which can take you way off track. **Meditation is not your creative brainstorming session.** Welcome all ideas to the surface, but anytime you get too far off into a particular idea, use your mantra to anchor back into the practice. If there's something that sticks with you after you're done meditating, then use your active, cognitive mind to investigate whether or not the idea would be appropriate for you to act upon.

And just because an idea isn't revolutionary doesn't mean it's not necessary for your growth. So don't disrgard the seemingly random ideas you remember after you're done meditating. Sometimes you will remember a person you need to call, a project you forgot to finish, or an item to add to your to-do list. Each of those seemingly insignificant ideas guides you toward the next step in your journey. Approach them with curiosity.

LOW-QUALITY QUESTIONS JUST GIVE YOU MORE EXCUSES.

MEDITATION IS NOT YOUR CREATIVE BRAINSTORMING SESSION.

"I MEDITATED, BUT NOTHING HAPPENED."

When you meditate with the expectation that something is going to happen, you're just setting yourself up for a disappointment. Sure, sometimes you will get huge sparks of inspiration, but the real benefits of meditation are seen in the macro, long-term outcome of your life trajectory. If you went to the gym three times, would you expect to get a six-pack of abs right away? No. It's a process. And although I've highlighted the importance of intention setting throughout this book, the goal of meditation is not to make things happen. The goal of meditation is to tune your nervous system to play in harmony with your life and to give yourself access to a field of unlimited potential and possibility. Set your intention and allow (do not force) it to unfold. Forcing it can quickly turn your meditation practice into an obsessive thinking practice. We do enough of that already. Meditation is about receiving, not searching. It's about listening, not talking.

Meditation is not an interrogation process with the universe.

Now that you have some new tools with which you can glean answers from meditation, let's practice.

GUIDED PRACTICE 15

Get the Answers You've Been Searching For

Time: 7 minutes

STEP 1   Start with the Freedom Trinity.

STEP 2   Ask a high-quality question.

STEP 3   Welcome your mantra into your mind using your favorite techniques.

MEDITATION IS NOT AN INTERROGATION PROCESS WITH THE UNIVERSE.

STEP 4 If any idea sticks with you after you're done meditating, write it down (even if it's not related to your original question). This is the beginning of your Divine Listening Journal. You can keep a physical journal of these ideas or jot them down in the notes on your phone. If nothing comes to you, don't worry. You can start your journal next time.

Essential Points from This Chapter

- Your life is always giving you the answers you need. Meditation tunes you to hear them.

- There's usually a feedback delay between when you ask a question and when you receive the answer.

- Don't ask the universe dumb questions. High-quality questions usually begin with "How . . . ?"

- Don't interrupt your meditation to write down ideas. Act only on the ideas you remember after your meditation is over.

- Intentions are important, but the goal of meditation is not to make things happen.

- Meditation is not an interrogation process with the universe.

CHAPTER

10

we build rituals

People would always ask my Baca for her recipes. She was a generous woman, so she would always share, but no one could ever quite replicate her cooking. It took me years of standing next to her in the kitchen to learn her secrets. The magic wasn't in the list of ingredients but in the subtle rituals that had been inherited and perfected through generations. It was in the unusual way she chopped onions in the palm of her hand instead of on a cutting board, how she let the butter sit out overnight and then mixed it with olive oil, how she flavored grease before she fried chicken, the way she insisted on mixing certain things with her hands instead of a utensil, and her ability to add just the perfect amount of shuga to everything to make it pop without being too sweet. These were her rituals.

Ritual connects us. It brings us together in a sacred space and helps us remember that we are not alone. It marks our lineage and builds a bridge between modern-day and ancient wisdom. The practice of ritual transcends culture, religion, and belief, and reminds us that we are part of the never-ending cycle of life. From birth to death, engagement to marriage, birthdays to proms, we use ritual to usher in life's most important moments. Humans have been doing rituals since the dawn of civilization, and science is finally catching up with what our ancestors have always known: rituals work. They help us feel connected to one another, they alleviate grief, they reduce anxiety before stressful events, and they help us perform better in life, at work, and in our passions.[1] But no rituals are more important than the ones we practice every day. I'm talking about the seemingly insignificant ones, like brushing your teeth, washing your face, and making your coffee in the morning. Our daily rituals are the most important ones because we do them most frequently. They create the patterns of our lives and over time become unbreakable habits. When was the last time you randomly forgot to brush your teeth in the morning? It just doesn't happen. And if you did forget to brush your teeth for some odd reason, I guarantee you would do whatever it took to fix your breath, even if it meant brushing with your finger, a napkin, or in the office bathroom.

I want the same thing to happen with your meditation practice. By turning meditation into a ritual and continuing to practice consistently, it will become an unbreakable habit, so much so that your day would feel incomplete without it.

THE THREE ESSENTIAL ELEMENTS TO BUILDING YOUR DAILY MEDITATION RITUAL

Every meditator needs to consider these three things when building a Daily Meditation Ritual:

1 **Time.** How long should you meditate? What time of day? What if you fall asleep? What if you're too busy?
2 **Place.** Where? What if you can't find peace and quiet? Should you listen to music while you practice?
3 **Shuga.** What's the special little something you add to your practice to make it unique to you?

Let's dive into each of them more deeply.

TIME

"How long should I meditate?"

People who never cook say they prefer eating out because cooking "takes too long." That's a myth. You can always whip something up for yourself much faster than scrolling through online menus and waiting for the food to be delivered. Cooking doesn't take as long as you think—and neither does meditation.

I find that it's better to *meditate daily for short amounts of time* rather than doing longer practices every once in while. Meditation is not a "whenever you have time" kind of thing. Practicing for five minutes every day is more beneficial than doing thirty-minute sessions twice a week.

My recommendation is to start meditating somewhere between ten and twenty minutes daily. My practices have fluctuated between five and thirty minutes over the years, but while you're first getting started, I don't recommend doing practices shorter than ten minutes because your body-mind system needs some time to warm up to the practice. You have to let the grease get hot before you fry the chicken (or tofu, if you're vegan).

People who run long distances know about a thing called "runner's high." The first part of a marathon is always the hardest, but beyond a certain threshold, exhaustion goes away and runners are blessed with a wellspring of energy. Meditation works similarly. If you're like me and have a superactive mind, you will notice that the first few minutes of your meditation are usually the toughest to get through: as soon as you sit down, the mind will start going wild. This is the cleaning process, which can sometimes feel chaotic. But after the mind has exhausted itself with all the overthinking, it will usually give up.

On days when you're feeling naturally relaxed, you might not have a threshold at all. On days when you're stressed and busy, you might stay restless for the entire practice. Your threshold will adjust with your life, but over time you will notice an average time it takes to start up your practice. Mine is seven minutes.

When I first started meditating, I only made time for five-minute practices—which is better than nothing—but I didn't really feel the magic of the practice until I pushed beyond that seven-minute threshold. Still today, even after years of meditating, my first seven minutes are like the beginning of an airplane ride: the takeoff is violent and turbulent, but after I get to a cruising altitude, I can take off my seat belt and explore the cabin of my mind.

Spend some time over the next week to see if you can find your personal threshold; then go beyond it. Not because longer meditations are better, but because it takes that much time for your brain to chill out. Even staying in meditation one or two minutes past your threshold is enough.

I've found that the sweet spot for most people is usually around twelve to seventeen minutes of total time meditating. But if you don't have that much time, it's okay. Don't judge the quality of your meditations on the basis of how long they are. The best thing to do is pick a length of time that fits in with the rest of your life. Once you pick a time, set a timer and stick to it. Refer back to our illustration of restfulness and restlessness in chapter 7. The box around the circle represents the

THE SWEET SPOT

FOR MOST PEOPLE IS USUALLY AROUND TWELVE TO SEVENTEEN MINUTES.

time commitment you set. Every fluctuation that occurs within the box is fair game. Even if you spend most of your time in a restless state, you will still notice the benefits after you're done meditating. Every experience is valuable.

"Help! I can't stop looking at the clock."

When I first started meditating, one of the most stressful things for me was watching the clock. I would compulsively open my eyes and look at the clock over and over and over, wondering how much time had elapsed. Thirty seconds can feel like five minutes when you're not used to sitting alone in silence. Instead of worrying about watching the clock, the best thing to do is to set a cooking timer. Although you might notice the feeling of anticipation when you set a timer too—wondering when it is going to ring, worrying that you forgot to set it, or checking to see how much time has passed—that's fine. It's totally normal. We are so accustomed to being bombarded with notifications all day that giving ourselves uninterrupted alone time can feel selfish, too long, or unusual. If the temptation to look at the clock becomes overwhelming, just give yourself permission to take a quick glance instead of forcing yourself not to—then use your mantra to bring yourself back. All that anticipation about the clock is just a mutated form of excitement, a yearning to step back into your life. Don't judge it. Feel it. Surrender to it. Allow it to be infused by the energy of your mantra. As you get more comfortable sitting in silence, that anxiety about the timer going off will subside, and you will actually begin to look forward to meditating longer.

"What time of day should I meditate?"

The annoyingly simple answer: whenever you want, except for immediately after you eat, because your body will be busy digesting food.

I personally love to meditate first thing in the morning, before I do anything else at all. I prefer a morning practice because it's my only chance to experience my natural energy before the rest of the world gets ahold of me. If you meditate before you have your coffee, before you have your tea, before you smoke your weed, before you have your wine, before you look at your to-do list, and especially before you look at your phone, then you will get to know the person underneath all of that stimulation.

CHECK YOURSELF BEFORE YOU CHECK YOUR PHONE.

Although I'm biased toward morning meditations, many of my clients like to meditate before they go to bed. That's also a great option; it just doesn't work for me because if I wait until nighttime, there is a chance I'll get too busy or tired and it won't happen. And if you're someone who likes to drink wine or smoke weed at night, you'll want to see how meditating under the influence impacts your practice. I find most people *think* they'll enjoy meditating stoned or tipsy but end up finding it counterproductive. You might instead consider meditating on your lunch break, when you get home from work, after the gym, before you pick up your kids from school, or before you go into the office.

Choose any time that works for you. Just make sure you get it in.

"What if I don't have time to meditate?"

People say they don't have time to meditate, but most of us are doing a ten-minute Instagram meditation every morning (or email/texting/Facebook/insert other app here).

Here's an easy way to change your life: check yourself before you check your phone.

What you experience in the first few minutes after you wake up has a consequential influence on your psyche, mood, and emotional state for the rest of the day. And this is not just some woo-woo spiritual stuff. Science has proven that when you wake up in the morning, your brain is in a similar state to that of hypnosis. Your mind is ultrapermeable and sensitive to all outside input. Every stimulus, thought, and emotion penetrates the brain more deeply in the moments just after waking up. So if one of the first things you see is a fear-mongering news article or an annoying email from a colleague who needs something or a notification that you overdrew your checking account last night, you are at risk of being negatively impacted for the rest of your day. Countless studies have been done on this, but few are more shocking than the findings researchers discovered about watching negative news: people who watched as little as *three minutes* of negative news in the morning were a whopping 27 percent more likely to report having a bad or unhappy day six to eight hours later.[2] What you experience in the morning sets the emotional trajectory for your entire day. So be sure to check in with yourself—with your own emotions, with your own sensations, with your own health, with your own desires, with your own aspirations—before you let outside influences check in with you.

Here are a few recommendations that can help you avoid getting into the phone zone in the morning:

1 **Get an alarm clock instead of using your phone to wake up.** There are some really cool (and cheap!) ones available both online and at your favorite brick-and-mortar stores.
2 **Make your bedroom a "no social media zone."** This will benefit more than just your meditation practice, especially if you have a special someone.
3 **Deactivate the notifications from your phone's lock screen.** This way, after you turn off your alarm, you won't see any alerts waiting for you. If you use your phone to listen to my guided meditations, turning off your notifications is even more important.

I have recommended this phoneless morning practice to thousands of people, so I know with certainty that it works. But I'll warn you now that you'll probably feel a bit of anxiety when you try to give it up. In a world where we often feel so alone, the desire to connect is strong. I feel it too. Take the ten minutes you would have wasted scrolling through your phone and spend it meditating instead.

Use that desire to connect with others and transform it—even just for a few moments—into an intimate connection with your Higher Self.

Meditation only takes a few minutes. You have time. You just have to commit.

"What if I fall asleep when I meditate?"

Then, as my dad would say when us kids were awake past our bedtime, "You betta take yo' ass to sleep." Meditating is an active and participatory practice, so if you can actually fall asleep during your practice, your body needs rest. Honor it. If you're having trouble sleeping, be sure to try out the guided minipractice in chapter 12.

"What do I do after I'm done meditating?"

Once your timer rings, try sitting with your eyes open or closed for another minute or two. Just give yourself a moment to process the experience. You can lie down, stretch, deepen your breath, or even move around a little bit. The most important thing is to give yourself a peaceful transition back into your busy life. Definitely wait at least a couple of minutes before you go back online. The end of your meditation practice is sacred—it's your chance to integrate wisdom from a higher source. It's the bridge between the worlds. Respect it.

PLACE

"Where should I meditate?"

You can sit anywhere you'd like. Remember, the first step of our Freedom Trinity is to "Sit yo' ass down . . . but comfortably"—so just make sure it's cozy. Try a few different spots to discover how changing positions and locations affects the quality of your meditation. You might try your couch, your balcony, your backyard, the floor with your back up against a wall, a chair, the bathtub, the shower, your car, your bed, or outside with your back resting on a tree. My good friend Jeremy recently confessed to me that he mediates on the toilet; really, the options are endless. Once you explore a few different spots, pick your favorite and claim that as your daily meditation zone. It's easier to get into a rhythm with your practice if you remove the challenge of choice. As time passes, you can try exploring different environments. I've gotten pretty good at meditating on airplanes, in Uber cars, and even on the New York City subway.

"What if it's too noisy where I live?"

You do not need peace and quiet to meditate. Sure, peace and quiet are nice, but they're a luxury and should not be a requirement for your practice. The typical image of a woman sitting in yoga pants totally alone on a mountaintop in blissful serenity is just as incongruent with most of our lives as an image of a bald monk in an orange robe sitting alone under a tree. While some people are blessed to be able to meditate in a tranquil environment, that is not the status quo. Many of us live in apartment buildings with noisy neighbors and roommates or in homes with cars driving by, airplanes overhead, TVs blasting in the next room, and ambulances screeching down the street. Do not let noise become an excuse for you to skip your practice. Instead, reframe noise as *the sound of community*. You are a part of that community. So don't try to block out the people, children, and animals that share this earth in close proximity to you. Their space, their needs, their favorite TV shows, their kids, and their actions are just as important as yours. In the age of iPhones and earbuds, we have become so insulated that we forget we belong to an actual community. Consider exploring how you can welcome the sounds into your experience. Dance with the car alarms, sway with the

> **THE END OF YOUR MEDITATION PRACTICE IS SACRED—IT'S YOUR CHANCE TO INTEGRATE WISDOM FROM A HIGHER SOURCE.**

sirens, let your breath sync with the sound of passing traffic. It's all part of the divine play.

You could also try inviting your kids, your partner, or your neighbors to meditate with you. If they're not interested, see if they'll give you a consistent ten to fifteen minutes of quiet at the same time every day to support your healing.

I don't want to be idealist here and say that you'll never experience annoying sounds. If there's something in your environment that is extremely bothersome, put on some headphones and play some music or white noise, or just wait and meditate later.

Don't demand total peace and quiet to engage in a consistent practice—you may never get it.

"Can I listen to music while I meditate?"

When you listen to music, you are giving artists and producers the keys to your mental state, so you have to be careful about using music in your meditation. The song you pick will shift the trajectory of your practice. Choosing the wrong song might take you down a rabbit hole you never needed to explore, while choosing the right song could enhance your experience perfectly.

DON'T DEMAND TOTAL PEACE AND QUIET TO ENGAGE IN A CONSISTENT PRACTICE—YOU MAY NEVER GET IT.

There are two ways to use music to supplement your meditation practice:

1 **Music to enhance:** Using upbeat music while you work out or slow ballads during a breakup are examples of using music to enhance your *already present*

mood and mind-set. The best way to do this is to curate a playlist that is congruent with what you're already feeling to prolong or deepen that emotion. For example, I often have trouble crying when I'm sad, but if I turn on a few '90s Mariah Carey ballads when I'm already in a tender mood, my sadness will intensify, and the tears will start pouring down my cheeks. In this case, my song selection helps me dive deeper into my already present sadness. This is all about selecting songs that will intensify, deepen, or heighten your already present state.

2 Music to shift: Using music to *induce a desired emotional state* is a second and powerful way to incorporate music into your meditation practice.[3] If I'm feeling anxious or depressed but I need to be on camera in an hour to give a motivational talk, I will turn on upbeat tribal house music, dance ecstatically around my living room, and then sit in meditation to shift the quality of my energy. In this case, the music is helping me dissipate the depression and cultivate positivity. When selecting a song, think about the mood or emotion you want to invoke and play it before or during your meditation practice.

Important note: DO NOT USE MUSIC AS AN AVOIDANCE STRATEGY. It's easy, especially as you are in the early stages of your practice, to slip into a habit of using music to sidestep challenging emotions. If you are not careful, music can end up becoming a crutch that prohibits you from creating a long-term practice.

Remember, the purpose of Freedom Meditation is to allow your natural rhythms to ebb and flow, so if you choose a song that's out of alignment with your organic energy, you may miss out on the transformation you really need.

Ultimately, I recommend getting comfortable meditating in silence and using music only occasionally, as a supplement.

I know it can be challenging to find quality music to listen to during meditation, so I have created a playlist on the *Stay Woke* website that was specifically designed to help you shift and enhance your energy as needed. Each song has a particular purpose and is tuned to precise energy frequencies to help supercharge your practice. This way you don't have to worry about

searching for music on your own, risk being tainted by low vibrational songs, or, worse, be subject to listening to cheesy nature sounds every time you meditate.

SHUGA

Shuga is that special little something you add to your meditation to make it your own.

For the rest of this chapter, I'm going to provide some optional techniques you can use to add a little shuga to your practice. The key word here is "optional." You will love some of the methods presented, but there may be others you don't resonate with. Some will feel amazing, and others may feel weird or cheesy. If you don't like one of my suggestions, skip it! Ultimately, I want you to create your own unique practice—to pick the things you like and forget the things you don't. By the time you are done reading this chapter, you will have built your Daily Meditation Ritual, one you can do on your own and that feels unique and authentic to you.

Adding too much shuga to your recipe will make it too sweet, so be sure to follow these golden rules to find the perfect balance:

- Don't make it complicated.
- Light something on fire.
- Get lucky.

Don't Make It Complicated

I've been blessed to witness some of the most beautiful rituals as I've explored different spiritual practices. Some include processions and flowers and intricate altars that take hours to build. And while those types of rituals are beautiful, they are best saved for special occasions.

If you make your ritual too complicated, you'll never do it.

I want your Daily Meditation Ritual to be as easy as brushing your teeth or taking a shower. Simplicity does not take away from the sacredness of your practice. One of the purposes of creating a ritual is to anchor meditation into your physical experience. When meditation becomes a *physical ritual* and not just a mental practice, your body builds a pathway to find its way back to center (which is especially useful on those days when you're a hot mess and can't rely on your mind to get you there).

Light Something on Fire

When we heat up any element, it transforms into something new. That's why fire represents transformation in most spiritual traditions.

Here are a few ways to include fire in your meditation practice.

Candles   The candle is a simple fire tool that has been used for centuries. You can use the same candle for every meditation until it runs out or grab a fresh tea light candle every day. I like to get prayer candles in glass jars (you know, the ones they use at church), but without any saints on them—they are supercheap and easy to find online or at your local dollar store. You might also grab your favorite scented candle, but just make sure it's a natural scent so you're not breathing in toxic chemicals during your meditation. Once you light your candle, set an intention on the flame and ask that a fire be ignited within you to transform your life.

Sage   The practice of burning dried sage originally comes from certain Native American traditions and can be used to clear energy. I used it for the first time when I moved into my college dorm room to clear any lingering bad vibes from the space. From that moment on, sage became an integral part of my life. Burning sage is particularly powerful for removing external negative energy, but it also clears the heaviness that festers inside your own mind. When you combine sage smoke with your mantra, you create a powerful force field of protection around you. Sage is reasonably inexpensive and easy to find at your local natural food store, hippie market, Whole Foods, or Amazon.

Use sage daily or anytime you feel bad juju following you around.

THE ONLY THING REQUIRED FOR YOUR PRACTICE IS YOU.

Palo Santo   My personal fave. *Palo santo* literally translates to "holy wood," and it comes from a sacred tree native to South America. While sage clears negative energy, palo santo enhances positive energy. It strengthens the connection between you and your Highest Self. I first learned about palo santo from my good friend Isaac Koren, who produced my first album with me. He burned palo santo before every recording session to enhance our creative connection. I felt the effect so strongly that I now use it before I do anything creative. Everyone who works with me will tell you that I carry palo santo with me all the time. I light it in the studio, before I record podcasts, before I write, before I go on stage, and especially before collaborating with other people. Important note: palo santo is becoming so popular that South America's rain forests are being destroyed by corporations cutting down trees to meet the market demand. There's nothing spiritual about ruining the planet. If you use palo santo, please be sure to get it from a sustainable source, which means the wood is only sourced from naturally fallen trees.

How to use sage and palo santo:
- Use a lighter, match, or candle to set the herb or wood on fire.
- Let the flame burn for ten to thirty seconds, then blow it out.
- A strong scented smoke will start to emerge from the embers. Let it linger. The magic is in the smoke.
- Allow the smoke to cleanse your spirit and your space.
- You can trace the outline of your body with the smoke, draw infinity symbols in the air, hold it near specific body parts, or just set it aside and let the smoke do its thing.
- The smoke should stop burning on its own after a few minutes. If it doesn't, just splash it lightly with some water. Don't get it too wet, though! Sage and palo santo only burn when dry.

Incense   Incense is a more commonly used energy tool that somehow does not carry the burden of spiritual taboo like sage and palo santo do in some traditions, yet the energetic benefits of incense are just as powerful. Scented incenses hold varying energetic properties. If you don't know which scent to buy, just go with whatever smells good. Your intuition will guide you.

Essential Oils   If lighting something on fire doesn't work where you live or if you're sensitive to smoke, try essential oils. I always use essential oils when I'm traveling and often include them in my daily ritual, especially if I need extra support balancing my emotions. Just be sure you use the highest-quality essential oils, because many oils on the market are mixed with toxic fragrances and diluted with unknown chemicals.

Sage, palo santo, incense, and essential oils take advantage of the power of smell, which we discussed in the 6S Thought Spectrum in chapter 5. The sense of smell is one of the most primitive of all human senses. Familiar scents can immediately pull your brain back to the original association. As soon as I smell palo santo, it relaxes me and connects me with my spirit because I've used it so frequently in my rituals. If you incorporate smell into your meditations, your body's intelligence will build a habitual connection between the scent and your practice.

Get Lucky

Although I wish for everyone reading this book to get laid sometime soon, that's not what I'm talking about in this section. This is about finding your *lucky charm*. Think of your lucky charm as a personal talisman, a chosen physical object that becomes a sacred part of your practice.

Your lucky charm does not need to be an item of spiritual significance. It doesn't matter if it's a crystal, a necklace, a photo, a cross, a *murti*, a Bible, tarot cards, a magic wand, or any other random object, just make sure it's something that represents what you're trying to cultivate in your life through the practice of meditation. I've even used my wireless microphone as a lucky charm when I was trying to source creative ideas for my tour. Choose anything that is meaningful for you. If you're having trouble thinking of something, refer back to your vision from chapter 2 and choose an item that represents the life you're trying to manifest.

Using your lucky charm is easy:

- After you light something on fire, grab your lucky charm and hold it to your heart.

- Continue holding your lucky charm as you initiate the Freedom Trinity.
- You can keep your lucky charm close to your heart or set it down as you proceed with your practice.

What about Crystals?

I love using healing crystals as a supplement to my meditation practice—they serve as great lucky charms. There are many different opinions about how crystals and stones work, and as with all energetic tools that require a little faith, no one really understands the full breadth of how crystals impact the human experience. My personal belief is that crystals use two powerful traits to initiate healing: beauty and intention.

Like beautiful sunsets, no two crystals are alike, and each one was perfectly crafted by nature. Looking at a crystal evokes a sense of awe—it's hard to look at a crystal without saying, "Wow." They make us curious. They make us remember that even in the darkest caves, there is beauty. When you bring that same sense of wonder to your meditation practice, you open to the ever-present opportunities that surround you.

Crystals also have the power to ground our intentions into a concrete physical form. In this way, holding a crystal is like holding your intention in your hand. Here are a few of my favorite crystals and their corresponding energetic and intentional properties.

- Amethyst: protection
- Clear quartz: clarity
- Rose quartz: love

- Citrine: abundance
- Fluorite: good decisions
- Carnelian: creativity

I know the items I discussed in this chapter, like sage, sustainable palo santo, essential oils, and healing crystals, can be hard to find in certain communities. If that's the case, don't worry—I got you covered. Check out the "Goodies" section in the back of this book if you need help finding the right ritual tools. But please remember, none of this fancy stuff is required for your practice. Never skip meditating just because you don't have any ritual tools handy. **The only thing required for your practice is *you*.**

YOUR SECRET RECIPE

Everyone's Daily Meditaton Ritual will look a little different. **Mine usually looks something like this:**

- How long: 20 minutes
- What time: 8:30 a.m.
- Where: sitting on the ground on my balcony
- Shuga: a candle, palo santo, essential oils, and a citrine crystal

As soon as my alarm rings, I wake up, brush my teeth, splash some water on my face, and walk sleepy-eyed out to my balcony to meditate. After saying a quick prayer of gratitude, I light my candle, set a clear intention, and burn the palo santo using the flame from my candle. I've been lighting palo santo every morning for years, so now my mantra immediately arises as soon as I smell its sweet scent. I alternate between several different essential oils and crystals when I meditate, depending on what I'm trying to cultivate in my life that day, but I most commonly use citrine, which is all about generating abundance. I sit on my balcony for fifteen to twenty minutes, rocking and swaying until my timer rings.

If I'm traveling (which is often), I get it in where I can. I still try to meditate first thing in the morning no matter what, but I'll practice on the bed of the hotel room or on the couch of my Airbnb. In those cases, I travel with a tiny box of crystals and use essential oils instead of burning palo santo.

AMBER's meditation ritual is luxurious:

- How long: 11 minutes
- What time: 8:30 p.m.
- Where: in the bathtub after her daughter goes to sleep
- Shuga: a candle, sage, roman chamomile essential oil, and a rose quartz

Amber loves taking baths and has committed to taking one every night—not just to meditate, but also to give herself a moment of self-care after a busy day of work and kids. She puts a couple of drops of roman chamomile essential oil in her bathwater to help her relax, burns sage to clear any stressful energy, holds a rose quartz crystal on her heart to active the power of love, and lights a candle as she says her evening prayer. Amber is trying her best to meditate every night, but sometimes she gets too exhausted, so her plan B is to meditate in her car while on her lunch break.

DAVID is trying to meditate in the morning:
- How long: 15 minutes
- What time: 10:15 a.m.
- Where: on the floor in his bedroom, with his back resting against the edge of the bed
- Shuga: a dollar-store devotional candle, palo santo, and a printout of the script he's been writing

David wakes up at 10:00 a.m. to walk his dog and then sits down to meditate. He started leaving his phone at home during the dog walk and can already feel how much of a difference it makes to avoid checking his phone until after his practice. He's been writing a script for a new web series, so he decided to use the printout of his script as his lucky charm in hopes of inspiring new ideas. He lights a devotional candle that he found at the local dollar store and burns palo santo at the beginning and end of each practice to create an energetic bridge between himself and the source of creativity. He doesn't like sitting still, so he sways from side to side with the rhythm of his breath until the timer rings.

LISA created something unique:
- How long: 30 minutes
- What time: 7:00 a.m.
- Where: on her patio
- Shuga: a lavender-scented candle and motivational quotes

Lisa loves motivational memes, so she had a great idea to print out a bunch of her favorite quotes and put them in a jar that she keeps on her patio table. She picks a new quote out of the jar every morning and uses it as a lucky charm to anchor her practice. She also loves the smell of lavender, so she found a large candle scented with lavender essential oil that she lights only in the morning during her practice. Lisa meditates for thirty minutes because her mind is superactive and it usually takes her about ten minutes to pass the initial threshold. She loves meditating outside—something about it makes her feel more peaceful and relaxed—but if it's too cold or the weather is bad, she just meditates on her couch instead.

JORDAN's finally getting the hang of things:
- How long: 15 minutes
- What time: before bed
- Where: in his bed
- Shuga: '90s RnB music

Jordan is a night owl and usually stays awake until two or three in the morning. He notices that his mind is most at ease in the middle of the night, so he likes to meditate just before going to sleep. He's been meditating in his bed but is a little worried because sometimes he dozes off, so he's considering sitting on his desk chair instead. Jordan isn't really into crystals or candles, but he loves music, so he plays some of his favorite '90s RnB songs on low volume in the background while he meditates, and it's working well for him. He's almost afraid to admit it, but for the first time ever, Jordan is actually starting to enjoy *meditation*.

Now it's your turn.

Creating Your Daily Meditation Ritual

Use the lines below to write out the secret recipe for your Daily Meditation Ritual. Remember, you can always change this later as your practice evolves.

- How long: _____

- What time: _____

- Where: _____

- Shuga: _____

_____

Essential Points from This Chapter

- The three essential elements of your Daily Meditation Ritual: time, place, and a pinch of shuga.

- It's more beneficial to meditate every day for short amounts of time than doing longer practices every once in while.

- Any time of day is fine for meditation, except for immediately after you eat.

- Justin's golden rules for creating your ritual: Don't make it complicated, light something on fire, get lucky.

- Never skip your meditation just because you don't have any ritual tools.

CHAPTER

11

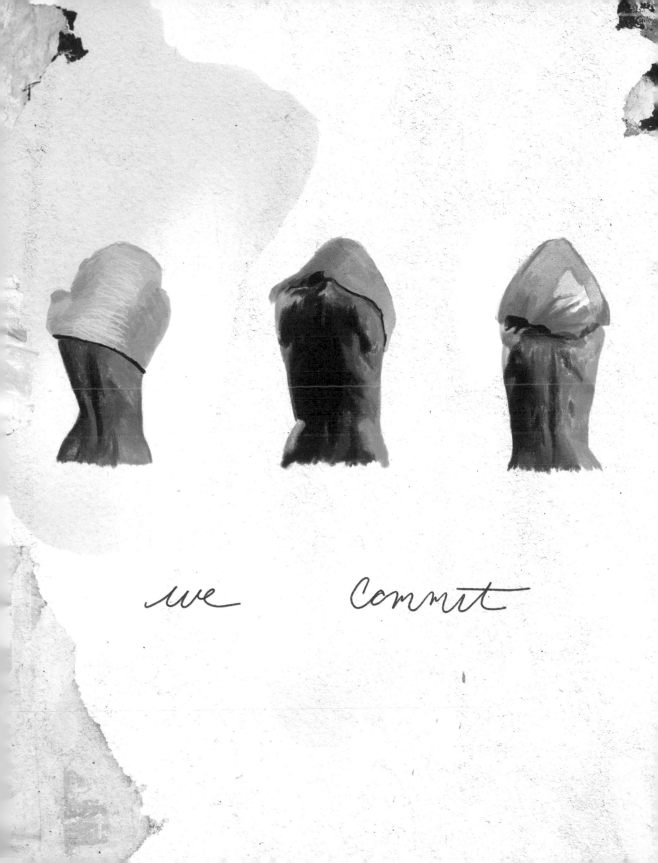

we   commit

The last ingredient in our recipe is the most important: commitment. I'm going to teach you exactly how to turn meditation into an unbreakable habit.

THE TRUTH ABOUT HABIT BUILDING

I want so badly to tell you that it will only take twenty-one days for you to create a habit out of meditation—that after twenty-one days of consistent practice, your entire life will change, and you'll be meditating every day without any resistance or distraction. But that would be a lie. It's a bit more complicated than that.

I hate to break it to you, but the notion that it takes twenty-one days to make or break a habit is a myth that has no scientific or quantifiable backing whatsoever. The rumor started with a paragraph in a 1960s book called *Psycho-Cybernetics* by plastic surgeon Dr. Maxwell Maltz. He observed that it took a minimum of twenty-one days for a person to get used to their new face after plastic surgery (notice the word "minimum"). This prompted Dr. Maltz to reflect on his own life, and he hypothesized that it also took him about twenty-one days to turn any new activity into a habit. Here's the quote that started it all: "These, and many other commonly observed phenomena tend to show that it requires a minimum of about 21 days for an old mental image to dissolve and a new one to jell."[1]

Psycho-Cybernetics went on to become a blockbuster hit, and your favorite self-help gurus took the number twenty-one and ran with it to the bank.

TO REACH FOR THE LIGHT.

This is capitalist oppression at its finest: giving you the false hope that your entire life can change within 21 days and then, when it doesn't, using your feeling of failure to sell you more products, more programs, more courses, and more books to chase the idea of perfection that has been carefully crafted to keep you trapped in the system. This system requires us to believe in the bullshit notion that we are all broken. We are not broken. Yes, we are dealing with some difficult matters in this lifetime, like systemic oppression, racism, environmental ruin, and the challenges of simply existing in daily life, but we are not broken. We are whole. We are perfectly imperfect and constantly evolving. And just because we have a desire to grow does not mean we are broken. **A flower is not broken just because it desires to reach for the light.**

The actual science behind habit building is much more empowering than the capitalist self-improvement myth. In 2009, Phillippa Lally and her team at University College London did a lengthy study to find the truth about forming habits.[2] Here's what they found:

- It takes anywhere from 18 to 254 days to form a new habit, depending on the type of activity and the motivations behind it. This means you can actually form a habit in *fewer* than 21 days.
- The average number of days to form a habit is 66.
- It's okay if you fall off track. It does not matter if you skip one day every once in a while. As long as you start up again quickly, there is no effect on the habit-formation process.

This is more reflective of our real lives: we try new things and fall off track. And every fall gives us valuable lessons, so that we can find our way back to center more and more quickly. I've fallen off track with my meditations many times over the years. There have been moments when I've forgotten my magic, when I thought I had to do it all alone, or when I've gotten "too busy." Luckily, life always has a way of nudging us back into alignment. Meditation ensures that you feel those nudges before they turn into bricks slamming you over the head.

Now that you know the science of habit building, it's time for the important part: commitment.

INTRODUCING: YOUR 40-DAY MEDITATION ~~CHALLENGE~~ *EXPERIMENT*

Think of this 40-day experiment less like a fix-your-life challenge and more like doing an anthropology study on yourself. Commit to the practice for 40 days, observe the findings, and draw conclusions based upon your results at the end of the experiment. If you see that your life has improved after the 40 days, continue with the practice. If you don't see a benefit at all, quit.

WHY 40 DAYS?

Based on the science, I could have chosen any number between 18 and 254, but 40 days feels short enough to be reasonable and long enough to require some commitment. Plus the number 40 has some spiritual significance. Lent is 40 days, the great flood mentioned in the Bible is 40 days, many yoga traditions practice 40-day initiations, a typical pregnancy lasts 40 weeks, black Americans were supposed to be given 40 acres and a mule as reparations after slavery. The significance of the number 40 is well documented throughout history, so I have always used the 40-day model to test out new practices in my own life.

If 40 days feels overwhelming, pick a different number that fits in with your life. Remember, you *always* have permission to change the recipe to suit your taste. Whatever you choose, though, commit to it! Don't blow yourself off. Pick a number of days that feels slightly longer than your comfort zone. If you pick too short of a time period, you'll miss the gifts and lessons that come with strengthening your commitment muscle.

The most important piece of advice I can give as you head into this new chapter of your life is to *be radically kind to yourself.* Meditation brings joy, purpose, and happiness, but it can also unearth pain and old wounds that never got a chance to heal. When that happens, don't be afraid to reach out for support—either from your community, a therapist, a healer, or me and my team. We have several resources available to you. See the "Goodies" section in the back of the book.

Meditation has transformed not only my life but also the lives of thousands of my students around the globe. You have all the ingredients now. Use my recipe as a guide, but be ready to experiment. I want this practice to fit in with your life so that it becomes an easy addition to your daily rituals. My greatest hope is that I receive a letter from you one day telling me how much your life was transformed by this practice. This is your opportunity now to take the reins, to be the change, to activate your vision, and to commit to YOU.

GUIDED PRACTICE 17

Your Customized Meditation ~~Challenge~~ *Experiment*

STEP 1   Commit to the practice for 40 days (or pick a different number that works for you).

STEP 2   Do your Daily Meditation Ritual every day. If you skip one day, it's okay—just begin the practice again immediately and continue the 40-day count.

STEP 3   Keep a Divine Listening Journal throughout the process to write about your ideas and experiences.

STEP 4   Mark your calendar for day 41. On this day, set aside an hour to reflect and journal about what you learned. Here are some important questions to consider at the end of your experiment:
1   What have you gained during these 40 days of commitment? Describe at least five things.
2   What positive qualities and habits have you cultivated during this process that you want to keep in your life as you move forward on your journey?

3 What do you have to gain by continuing on this path?

4 What more do you need to learn?

5 In what ways have you gotten closer to reaching your goals? How has your vision begun to manifest? Do you need to adjust it?

6 What's up with all those toxic patterns? Are there any new habits, people, thoughts, or beliefs that need to be released?

7 What do you need to adjust about your Freedom Meditation recipe to make your practice even more authentic and powerful for you?

8 Do you want to create a new ~~challenge~~ *experiment* for yourself? If so, what? Set a new number of days for your commitment.

Remember, this is *your* practice. Don't give yourself too many rules. Have fun. And watch the transformation unfold.

The very last time I saw my Baca alive was the hardest. I kneeled down next to her bed and said, "What am I going to do without you?" In her weak and frail voice, she looked me in the eyes and said, "All you have to do is think of me, and I'll be right there, baby."

Now that she's gone, I rely on the recipes she wrote on the backs of those old envelopes, the precious jewels of the Williams family heirloom. The scribbles on those envelopes, stained with grease and covered in crumbs from our years of cooking together, keep me on track whenever I get lost.

Baca's legacy lives on. And I hope that by your reading this book, her wisdom is inside of you, too.

I would've never imagined, all those years ago sitting on the beach with Lorin, that I would end up teaching meditation. I had never seen someone like me teaching this practice. But now, as I look around, I smile as we witness people of all identities, colors, ages, shapes, and economic backgrounds claiming their rightful throne in the new healing movement. There is a truth and reconciliation happening. We are breaking barriers and giving birth to a new generation of healers, leaders, and change makers.

This is the revolution. It starts inside. And it begins with you.

This is Freedom Meditation.

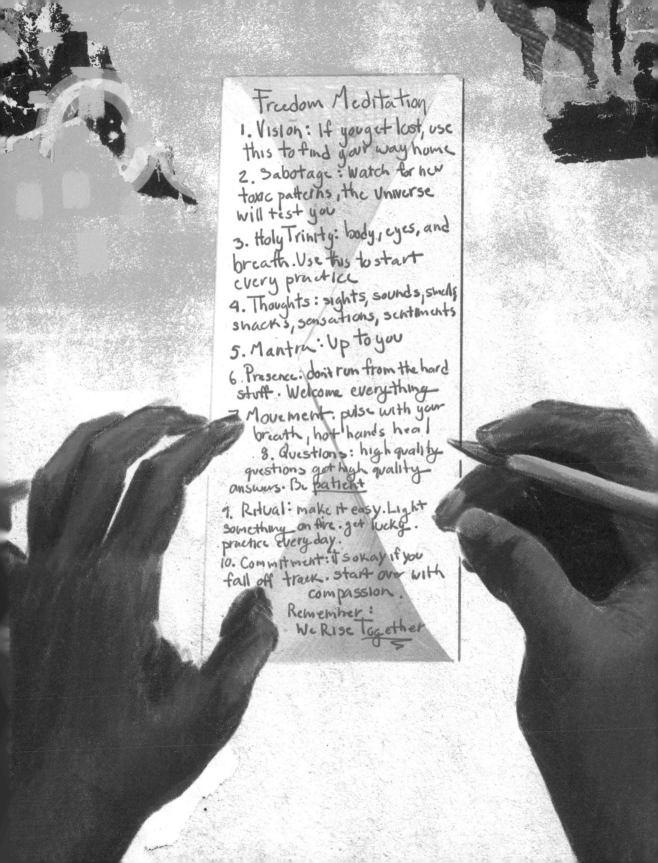

practices for your

Life:

33 rituals for deep awakening

As I wrote this book, I kept asking myself one question: *What do I wish I would've known sooner?* The answer to that question gave birth to the final part of *Stay Woke*: "Practices for Your Life." Here you will find thirty-three guided minipractices specifically designed to help you with:

- Productivity
- Purpose
- Anxiety
- Stress
- Sleep
- Focus
- Intuition
- Self-love
- Social justice

Part 2 builds upon everything you learned in part 1 and takes it to the next level, showing you how to apply meditation to specific areas of your life. Each minipractice has a motivational story or how-to teaching, an anchor mantra to help you explore unfamiliar dimensions of your practice, a guided meditation, and some optional journal prompts with which to process your emotions and, most importantly, inspire meaningful action in your life.

There are three ways to make the most of this section:

OPTION 1 When you have a particular issue you need help with, you can look through the table of contents and choose a minipractice for just that purpose. Think of it like a grab-and-go buffet: take what you like and leave what you don't. If you need a specific kind of healing or if you're going through a challenging situation in your life and you need some extra support, one of these minipractices will help.

OPTION 2   Let your intuition lead the way. Close your eyes, set an intention, flip open to any random page, and trust that you will be shown the practice that you need. This is one of my favorite techniques.

OPTION 3   If you want a more structured way to experience all of the guided minipractices, I've created a Daily Practice Plan to coincide with your 40-Day Freedom Meditation Challenge *Experiment*. The Daily Practice Plan has been thoughtfully curated to align and empower you, starting with strategies for overcoming stress and anxiety, then moving to growing your confidence, creativity, and power, and ending with ways to tackle social justice issues so we can create a better world. You can find the Daily Practice Plan on page 294.

Keep this book near your meditation space. Every question, every word, every mantra, and every story is here to serve you. When you can't find your way, these practices will guide you home.

These are Practices for Your Life.

CHAPTER

12

meditations for anxiety and stress

'Il never forget the day I drank two cold brews followed by eight shots of espresso and fell asleep immediately after. In that moment, I knew I had a problem.

Many of us are so used to operating in an underlying state of stress that we don't even realize it's happening. Anxiety has become the new norm. When we're overwhelmed with stress, we take vital energy away from the things that matter—our relationships, our families, our dreams, and our passions.

I know life can be a mess sometimes.

This chapter will help.

HOW TO STOP OBSESSIVE THINKING

ANCHOR MANTRA

"I see the truth. I choose the truth. I am the truth."

We've all been there: replaying a situation over and over in your head like a broken record, replaying conversations, creating hypothetical situations, asking your friends to validate your feelings—you know the drill. Obsessive thoughts can pull you off track for hours, days, or even weeks, distracting you from your purpose and wasting valuable energy that you could be using toward something more productive.

Obsessive thinking is the devil's meditation. It blinds you to truth and hooks your mind on the broken promise of "What if . . . ?" In these situations, we often suffer from two things:

1 Believing the hypothetical story we make up in our heads instead of *honoring the facts*

2 Getting so hooked on the hypothetical story that we avoid our *real* feelings

Imagine you meet someone new and start dating them casually. At first, you're texting each other all day, with rapid-fire responses and sweet messages of "Good morning" and "Good night." Then, all of a sudden, things shift. Your love interest starts responding more slowly. An entire day goes by without much communication, and your brain goes wild. You see them liking and commenting on other people's photos online, so why aren't they responding to you? Maybe they met someone new? Maybe you said something to offend them? You start replaying every conversation in your head. Rereading your text history, searching for flaws in your communication. Maybe you were too much? Too clingy? Too vulnerable? You call your best friend to get some advice, and they remind you that "he wasn't shit anyways" and that, after all, you deserve better. He was probably a liar, a cheater, or maybe "the universe was just protecting you."

Sound familiar? I've been there too, many times. And this kind of obsessive thinking isn't just relegated to dating. It also happens at work, with friends, and with family.

Any time you're in this situation, I want you to close your eyes, take three deep breaths, and fill in these blanks:

These are the facts: _____.

This is what I'm making up: _____.

By getting hooked on this hypothetical story, I am avoiding feeling:

_____.

Maybe it's rejection, loneliness, or abandonment that you're avoiding. Or maybe it's sorrow, anger, or simply admitting to being wrong. Either way, the hypothetical story is just a distraction from your growth.

Most of us create hypothetical stories because we want to manipulate situations to lean in our favor or so that we can make sense of what's happening—especially if it's not what we hoped for or expected. But this is not a time to run away from reality. That just creates more pain. The way through the challenge is to *accept what is*.

If you're already spiraling and you've started calling your friends to ask what they think about a situation or started creating different conspiracy theories, I want you to stop now and do this guided practice right away.

The Practice

Place your hands over your heart, close your eyes, take five deep breaths, and begin your Freedom Meditation practice using the anchor mantra "I see the truth. I choose the truth. I am the truth." (If you're in a triggered state, I recommend using the guided audio practice, which you can download for free on my website.)

After you are done meditating, use the journal prompts below to help you move through the situation. Rinse and repeat as needed.

If you prefer to be guided through the audio version of this experience, go to justinmichaelwilliams.com/staywoke.

JOURNAL PROMPTS

Think of a moment that triggered you, then answer the following questions:

1 What are the facts? What do you know *for sure*?
2 What is the hypothetical story you're making up about this situation?
3 What emotion are you avoiding feeling by holding on to this story?
4 Is there something you can Google, watch, or research to help you process the emotion you're avoiding? Spend time doing that instead of obsessing over the story. That's where the real healing begins.

WHEN YOU'RE STRESSED ABOUT MONEY . . .

ANCHOR MANTRA

"I am ready to receive. Abundance, come to me."

I mentioned earlier in the book that *money does buy happiness*—at least up to a certain dollar amount. Studies have proven that until your basic needs are met, money is vital to happiness for everyone. But after that, the emotional value of money drops drastically.[1]

Most self-help gurus will tell you not to focus on money but, rather, to pursue your passions over profit. And while I think that's a great approach for people who are financially stable, it doesn't work for everyone. If you're stressed about how to pay your bills, you'd be better off securing some bags. And you don't have to feel bad about it.

When I first started my marketing business, my finances were a total roller coaster. One month I would be buying bougie organic green juices and the next month I'd be saying a prayer at the checkout stand, knowing damn well my account was overdrawn but hoping my card wouldn't be declined so I could buy a ten-pack of the blue ramen noodles. I wouldn't wish that level of stress upon my worst enemy.

Never be ashamed of your desire for money, especially if you're having a hard time financially. Without money, it's impossible to thrive in our modern society. Your desire for it doesn't make you greedy or bad. But please remember, money is not your god. It's a resource for you to use—not something to worship or praise.

Pro tip: The way you *spend* your money has a greater impact on your happiness than how much you have stored in the bank. If you're low on cash and you want to get happier, stop wasting your money on material things and focus on buying experiences that connect you with the people you love.[2]

The purpose of the following practice is to provide you with two things: (1) a meditation to help you relax when you're stressed about money and (2) some ideas on how to make more money if you need to.

The Practice

If you're feeling stressed about money, the most important thing to do is slow down your breath to relax your nervous system.

Start with the 6 Count Breath: inhale for 6 counts through the nose, hold the breath in for 6 counts, then exhale for 6 counts through the mouth. Repeat this ten times, then immediately drop into your Freedom Meditation practice using the anchor mantra "I am ready to receive. Abundance, come to me."

If you prefer to be guided through the audio version of this experience, go to justinmichaelwilliams.com/staywoke.

JOURNAL PROMPTS

After your nervous system settles, use the tips below to start changing your financial situation. Remember, you aren't going to make more money by just sitting and thinking about it. You must take action.

1 If you let your guard down and become vulnerable, is there someone you can call to ask for support (either for financial help or just for advice on how to make more money)?

2 What are three things you could stop spending money on to help you save?

3 How else might you make more money outside of your primary source of income? Multiple streams of income are necessary for most of us these days, myself included. The average millionaire has seven streams of income. You can join the gig economy by renting out a room in your house, driving for a ride-sharing service, doing odd jobs through an online referral service, or becoming a virtual assistant or online freelancer. You might also look into selling a product you believe in through a multilevel marketing company. Although MLM gets a bad rap because of some companies' unethical practices, many companies do offer great products and a legitimate source of income.

MONEY IS NOT YOUR GOD. IT'S A RESOURCE FOR YOU TO USE—NOT SOMETHING TO WORSHIP OR PRAISE.

I trained myself to function on very little sleep at a young age. In high school, I worked at Starbucks in the mornings starting at 4:30 a.m., got to school for student government at 7:00 a.m., and had after-school band practice until 5:00 p.m. After band, I would do homework, chat on AOL Instant Messenger, browse through Myspace, watch porn after everyone went to bed (which downloaded painfully slowly in the early 2000s), and finally go to sleep around midnight or 1:00 a.m., only to start the process all over again the next day.

My late-night tendencies persisted through my late twenties. I prided myself on excelling in school and work on just a few hours of sleep, bragging about how I was "most creative" at 2:00 a.m. and feeling superior to "morning people" who claimed to wake up at sunrise.

Then I found out I was doing it all wrong.

I always thought sleeping less meant I was getting more done—but that's not the way it works. Sleep-deprived people are proven to be less productive, less creative, less attentive, more moody, more likely to be obese, have poorer decision-making skills, and are more likely to overreact to negative experiences than people who sleep well. I don't know about you, but I don't want any of those words to describe me. So I decided to do an experiment. I committed to an average of seven to eight hours of sleep per night for six months to see if it would make any difference. The results were wild. I ditched caffeine altogether after a fifteen-year daily habit, yet I could still pull the occasional all-nighter as needed without any stimulants. My emotions became more regulated; I had fewer days where I woke up in a bad mood for no apparent reason. My workouts were stronger, my dreams were more vivid, my mind was more focused, but most importantly, I felt creatively stimulated all day on my *own natural energy*.

The studies were right—this sleep thing works.[3]

I understand that for some people losing sleep is not a choice. You want to sleep more, but you can't because you're anxious or stressed. When that happens you feel like you "might as well do something productive" rather than tossing and turning all night. Or maybe you don't do anything productive at all, but you end up scrolling through your feed or online shopping in the middle of the night, only to wake up in the morning feeling groggy and irritated. If that sounds like you, you're not alone: one study found that an astounding 85 percent of US workers lose sleep because of work-related stress.[4]

Whether you have trouble sleeping because of stress or simply want to uplevel your sleep game, the following practice can help.

The Practice

This practice is called the Breathing Body Scan. I recommend using the accompanying audio guide from the *Stay Woke* website, especially if you're new to this technique. You can also use the condensed script below to guide yourself through the practice.

- Lie down on your back, arms by your sides, with the palms of your hands turned up and your feet flopped out to the side.
- Get comfortable so you don't have to move too much.
- Take a few deep breaths.
- Repeat to yourself mentally, "I am allowed to let go."
- Begin to scan your body, starting from your feet and working up to your head. Bring awareness to each body part for 5–10 seconds. For example: Bring awareness to the sensation in your right foot for 10 seconds, then your left foot. Then your right calf muscle, followed by your left calf muscle. Then your right thigh, then the left thigh. Work your way up the body until you get to the top of your head.
- After you bring awareness to each part of the body, take twenty-five deep breaths. Count all twenty-five breaths to yourself mentally.

If you prefer to be guided through the audio version of this experience, go to justinmichaelwilliams.com/staywoke.

Sometimes you will fall asleep midway through the body scan—that's great! But other times you will not. If you don't fall asleep, don't worry—you're not doing it wrong. The purpose of the Breathing Body Scan is to help you relax your mind so that you can sleep more easily. After the scan, do your best not to get on your phone or turn on any bright lights; those can delay or interrupt your sleep cycle.

JOURNAL PROMPTS

1 What thoughts keep you up at night?
2 What are you usually doing the hour before bedtime? How might this be affecting your sleep?
3 Is there something relaxing you can try doing for the next seven days to replace your usual presleep activities? Write it down.

FORGET ABOUT WORK/LIFE BALANCE

"I deserve this moment."

It was Saturday night, and there I was . . . working until 2:00 a.m., binging on Sour Patch Kids, and complaining to my friend Cristi about my lack of work/life balance. Then she said some words of wisdom that changed my perspective completely: "Justin, you actually *do* have work/life balance. It just doesn't fit the traditional model."

The traditional model looks something like this: You drive to work in rush hour traffic at 8:00 a.m., talk to your mom on the phone at lunch, get off at 5:00 p.m., drive to happy hour, watch Netflix, eat dinner, maybe have sex (if you're lucky), and go to bed. Every day is a sweet balance of work and rest. If you're not on the clock, you don't think about work. And weekends are yours for the taking— popping into a yoga class, drinking bottomless mimosas at Sunday Funday, and ignoring your work emails until you're back in the office on Monday morning.

Cristi was right. Trying to impose that model of work/life balance on my life was like Cinderella's evil sister trying to put her big-ass foot in that teeny-tiny shoe: it just didn't fit.

If you have a side hustle, a passion project, or a job that requires more than eight hours of your day, then you need a new model of work/life balance. A model that expands and contracts with your life and takes into consideration that you might actually *enjoy* the work that you do.

My model is a little more like a pendulum. I swing between periods of intense focus and rebellious abandon. Sometimes I work from ten to fourteen hours per day, but after a few weeks, I always give myself time to completely disconnect. I love retreating to nature, and my friends know I'm the king of turning my phone on airplane mode and playing hooky at the Korean spa on a random Wednesday.

I believe people strive for better "work/life balance," not because they work too much, but because they have trouble disconnecting from work when they're done. We've all been there—those times when you can't stop checking your inbox even though you're supposed to be on vacation or when you end up complaining about your coworkers at a romantic dinner with your partner.

What you need in those situations isn't work/life balance. You need a tool to help you disconnect from work more easily, so that when you're ready to put it down, work doesn't bleed into your life, your relationships, and your sleep.

That's where Freedom Meditation comes in.

Mindfulness trains you to be in the moment, fully immersed in exactly what you're doing right now. One way to practice this is through the process of savoring. Think of it like letting a piece of chocolate melt in your mouth slowly rather than chewing it up and swallowing it real quick. You can do this with your life experiences as well. Research has proven that when we savor our positive experiences, our happiness levels rise in both the short and the long term.[5]

Use this practice to strengthen your in-the-moment muscle so that you can be more fully present instead of being lost in a sea of unwelcome thoughts about work. **Don't miss out on another precious moment by being clocked in to work without getting paid**.

The Practice

Train your focus and awareness by starting your practice with the Double Down Breathing technique. It's easy:

- Inhale for 1 count, then exhale for 2 counts.
- On the next breath, inhale for 2 counts, then exhale for 4 counts.
- On the third breath, inhale for 3 counts, then exhale for 6 counts.
- Continue this pattern (exhales are double the length of each inhale) until you get to 8 counts for your inhale and 16 counts for your exhale.
- Then reverse the count, going backward until your inhale is a count of 1.

After you finish the breathing practice, start your Freedom Meditation Practice, breathing normally. Use the anchor mantra "I deserve this moment."

If you prefer to be guided through the audio version of this experience, go to justinmichaelwilliams.com/staywoke.

JOURNAL PROMPTS

1 What does an ideal model of work/life balance look like to you?
2 How does being overwhelmed by your thoughts about work impact your personal life?
3 In what moments could you benefit from completely disconnecting from work? List them. Remember, you can use Freedom Meditation and the Double Down Breathing technique to deepen your level of presence prior to any of the moments you list.

ANCHOR MANTRA

"Just like me, this person has suffered. Just like me,
this person has pain. May we both find peace."

Look—I get it. Your parents stress you out sometimes. And the phrase "They're doing the best they can" just seems like an excuse at this point. But **try not to be so upset when your parents don't meet your expectations. Hell, you didn't meet all of theirs either. Give your parents a break.**

That doesn't mean you absolve them of accountability, and I'm certainly not suggesting you tolerate abuse. But before you let anger and irritation boil your blood, try to put yourself in their shoes. Imagine them as a child. Think about their trauma. Think about their pain, much of which has never been healed or processed.

I know you have a dream of buying your mom or dad their dream house or surprising them with that dream car one day—but what could you do to make their life easier now? Instead of looking to your parents to see what they can do for you, ask what you can do for them sometimes. Instead of always expecting them to give, and show up, and be available, and say the right things, give them an opportunity to take, rest, relax, and make mistakes.

Next time you get triggered by your parents, try this compassion-based meditation practice. Compassion practices are known to increase understanding and empathy and to make us happier. This is one of my favorites.

**TRY NOT TO BE SO UPSET
WHEN YOUR PARENTS
DON'T MEET YOUR EXPECTATIONS.
HELL, YOU DIDN'T MEET
ALL OF THEIRS EITHER.**

The Practice

STEP 1   Place a hand over your heart and close your eyes.

STEP 2   Picture one of your parents as a child. Visualize them as clearly as possible. What are they wearing? What expression is on their face? What do they smell like? How does this visualization make you feel? Welcome all emotions. Keep breathing deeply.

STEP 3   Now think about how they've suffered in their life. Imagine their fears, and conflicts, and losses, and failures, and heartbreaks.

STEP 4   Initiate the anchor mantra "Just like me, this person has suffered. Just like me, this person has pain. May we both find peace." Continue visualizing your parent as a child as you breathe. On each exhalation, send the energy of this compassion-based mantra to the child version of your parent.

If you prefer to be guided through the audio version of this experience, go to justinmichaelwilliams.com/staywoke.

JOURNAL PROMPTS

1 What do you imagine your parent's emotional health was like when they were young? What were their struggles? What kept them awake at night? What dreams did they abandon? What were their traumas?

2 Given your responses to the previous question, why do you think they are the way they are now?

3 Is there something you can do to help your parent today? Something to make their life a little easier? It can be simple. Sometimes a text message is all it takes.

HOW TO MANAGE NERVOUSNESS AND FEAR

ANCHOR MANTRA

"You got this."

I can give a motivational talk in front of thousands of people with very little nervous energy, but sometimes when I have to sing I get totally taken over by anxiety. I can't think straight, I feel disconnected from my body, and I even start to tremble a bit. It reminds of being in gospel choir in eighth grade when I got asked to sing a solo. I stood up in front of the room, and just as the choir director played the intro to the song, my fear kicked into overdrive. My heart started pounding, my hands got shaky, my jaw got tight. I hoped nobody could tell I was getting nervous, but the feeling intensified until my right leg started shaking so badly that I literally had to grab my foot and finish the entire song standing on one leg.

For me, singing is the trigger; for you, it might be something else. Maybe it's public speaking. Maybe it's dancing, auditions, or giving a presentation at school or work. Whatever it is, disarming your nerves is essential to your creative evolution.

The practice I'm sharing with you here is what I use in my own life every time I get nervous to step on stage. Admittedly, it won't take your nerves down to zero, but a 60 percent decrease makes a big difference when your anxiety is through the roof.

The first step is ecstatic shaking and dancing. Don't do choreography or anything like that; just close your eyes and let the body's natural intelligence move you. Be as big and dramatic as possible. When you're nervous, you can usually feel the energy of it metastasizing in certain areas of the body. The key is to let it circulate and release. Yes, you'll look a little crazy, but who cares? I even do this in the bathroom sometimes before I go on stage. A few of my favorite songs for shaking it out are "Afrovita (Original Mix)" by Iñaky Garcia, "Dreams and Nightmares" by Meek Mill, and "Clap the Buka" by Harem.

The next step, and this is the most important, is to remember that when you believe there are no consequences, it's easier to rest in your natural creative flow. Think about it. When you're alone in your car and no one is listening or watching, don't you feel like you could've been a top contestant on *American Idol*? That's because you allow yourself to get into a state of flow. When you aren't focused on the results, you aren't as self-critical, so it's easier to access your creative energy. You need to mimic that scenario next time you're nervous to share. Remind yourself: this is not brain surgery. The consequences likely won't be as severe as you're making them out to be.

The fear of discomfort stops us from sharing our gifts far too often. It makes me sad to count the times I've withheld sharing my voice for fear of experiencing my nerves. My hope is that this practice will help you manage your fear and nervousness so that you can say yes to your creative flow.

The Practice

First, throw on one of your favorite upbeat jams—something with drums usually helps—and dance/shake it out to move the stagnant energy. After you exhaust yourself, stop the music, stand completely still, close your eyes, and feel the current of energy moving through your body.

Then take several deep breaths and initiate the anchor mantra "You got this." Affirming your power, affirming your courage, affirming your strength. You may not get to the purest state of 100 percent confidence, but you will definitely feel an energy shift. This new energetic space is where the best version of you is born. This is where flow comes from. This is where excellence comes from. This is the womb of creative connection. Stay in that space as long as you can.

If you prefer to be guided through the audio version of this experience, go to justinmichaelwilliams.com/staywoke.

JOURNAL PROMPTS

1 What consequences are you making up in your head? Call them out.

2 If all of those consequences came true, what would actually happen? What's the worst-case scenario?

3 What's the best-case scenario?

4 Can you think of a time when you were nervous about something and it ended up not being that big a deal? Write about it.

5 What can you remind yourself of when your nerves kick back into overdrive?

GRATITUDE TO SHIFT YOUR MOOD

ANCHOR MANTRA

"Thank You."

Most people think, "When I'm happy, then I'll be grateful." But that's not the way it works. Gratitude is the gateway to happiness, not the other way around.

The reason we call it a gratitude *practice* is because sometimes you have to force it to feel it. When you write down something you have to be grateful for or express gratitude out loud to a friend, you allow the energy of gratitude to move through you. As gratitude circulates through your energy field and onto paper or out of your mouth, the by-product—happiness—will reverberate through your system. This is especially helpful when life gets tough. In the moments when you're feeling at your lowest, you can always turn to a gratitude practice to elevate your mood.

People who have a regular gratitude practice experience less depression and are more resilient following traumatic life events. They're also healthier, both physically and psychologically; they get more restful sleep, and they experience less fatigue and burnout. One of my favorite studies on gratitude found that heart failure patients who kept a gratitude journal for eight weeks showed reduced signs of inflammation afterward.[6] Gratitude heals your body on a cellular level.

The following practice was created to help you cultivate gratitude. Anytime you're feeling stressed, angry, or upset, you can return to this practice to brighten your spirit.

GRATITUDE IS THE
GATEWAY TO HAPPINESS.

The Practice

Place your hands over your heart, take five deep breaths, and softly whisper the words "Thank you, thank you, thank you" for 30 seconds to a minute. Then begin your Freedom Meditation practice, but replace your usual mantra with the suggested anchor mantra, "Thank you."

As you repeat the mantra, welcome all thoughts to your mind. If stressful energy arises, remember, it just wants to be bathed, soothed, and released by the energy of gratitude. Allow it all to come forward.

After your timer rings, complete the following journal prompts.

If you prefer to be guided through the audio version of this experience, go to justinmichaelwilliams.com/staywoke.

JOURNAL PROMPTS

1 Write down three *specific* things you have to be grateful for today. Pro tip: One of the biggest mistakes people make when writing a gratitude list is being too general. If you're too general, you'll get bored. That's why I say, be specific.

2 Send a quick text message or email to someone you're grateful for. Share from your heart, expecting nothing in return.

3 Write a sincere gratitude letter to God, the universe, or whatever Higher Power you believe in, thanking them for the joy in your life. You can also close your eyes and say a gratitude prayer directly to your Higher Power instead of writing it down.

FAKING HAPPINESS CAN HURT YOU.
DO THIS INSTEAD . . .

ANCHOR MANTRA

"It's okay. I am allowed to feel."

In the era of motivational memes and untrained life coaches, happiness has become trendy. But science is proving that striving for too much happiness can actually be bad for you.[7] I know it sounds counterintuitive, but picture this . . .

It's Friday night after a long workweek, and you're exhausted and a little moody, but your friends are ready to turn up. You don't really want to go out, but YOLO, so you take a couple of puffs off your vape pen, put on something cute, and give yourself a pep talk in the mirror (when really you just want to lie in bed and watch Netflix). Once you arrive at the club, the bouncer is rude, the drinks are weak and too expensive, and the music is just a little too techno for your liking. The look on your face tells everybody you aren't feeling it, but you try to fake it—buying more drinks, forcing yourself to have fun—all the while wishing you would've just stayed home. The harder you try to be happy, the more irritated you get. Your friends seem to be having the time of their life, so why aren't you? Why do you always get in these moods for no reason? You always say you want to go out and do fun things, so what's the problem? The guilt kicks in. You spend the rest of the night in a mental tug-of-war with yourself, until it's finally late enough for you to go home without anyone questioning it.

This is an assault on your emotional health.

Emotional health does *not* mean *always being happy*. In fact, studies have shown that faking a smile is more detrimental to your emotional health than feeling sad. So next time you're in a bad mood, don't feel so guilty about it—a gratitude practice isn't always necessary. Sometimes the way to feel better is by welcoming your emotions without judgment. Emotional balance means being able to paint with every color on the palette—including the feelings that aren't so pleasant.

Meditation invites you to welcome all of your thoughts, feelings, sensations, and emotions without judgment, which leads to better psychological health overall.[8]

The next time you're in a funk, try this practice.

The Practice

Take five deep breaths, in through your nose and out through your mouth. Place your hands over your heart and begin your Freedom Meditation practice using the anchor mantra "It's okay. I am allowed to feel."

If you prefer to be guided through the audio version of this experience, go to justinmichaelwilliams.com/staywoke.

JOURNAL PROMPTS

1 Take five deep breaths and complete these sentence stems:

"Right now I feel _____ ."

"I want to avoid this feeling because _____ ."

"If I allowed myself to fully experience this emotion,

it would say _____ ."

"If I *really* allowed myself to experience this emotion without holding back,

it would say _____ ."

2 What action could you take right now that would honor your emotions? Remember, you have permission to cancel, change plans, or rearrange your schedule. Just because you're free doesn't mean you're available.

JUST BECAUSE YOU'RE FREE DOESN'T MEAN YOU'RE AVAILABLE.

THE POWER OF AWE

"I am connected to all that is. I am part of the Great Mystery."

I was introduced to the concept of awe as a science by my soul brother, mentor, and friend Dacher Keltner, the founding director of the Greater Good Science Center at UC Berkeley. We've all experienced awe. It's in the moments when your jaw drops to the floor, when you get goose bumps, or when tears of amazement stream down your cheeks.

Awe is the wonder of a newborn baby.

Awe is admiring a beautiful sunset.

Awe is watching Beyoncé perform at Coachella or listening to Oprah's acceptance speech at the 2018 Golden Globes.

Awe reminds us of the miracle of life—that we are all connected to something greater. It puts things into perspective; minor, everyday concerns never seem all that serious once you realize that it's all part of the Great Mystery.

Science is proving that the benefits of awe don't just last for a few minutes; they reverberate through our lives, bringing forth a renewed sense of gratitude, creativity, happiness, and connectedness to others. If you want to expand your capacity for joy, happiness, and life satisfaction, then turn your awareness toward awe.[9]

The Practice

You don't even need leave your home to experience awe—watching a YouTube video will do the trick! Search for things like nature videos or motivational speeches, or just type the phrase "top awe-inspiring videos" in the search bar if you can't think of anything.

Once you pick a video, watch it with the full presence of all your senses. Indulge. Be present with every emotion that arises.

After it's over, drop into your Freedom Meditation practice right away, using the anchor mantra "I am connected to all that is. I am part of the Great Mystery."

If you prefer to be guided through the audio version of this experience, go to justinmichaelwilliams.com/staywoke.

JOURNAL PROMPTS

This journal prompt is adapted from the Greater Good Science Center at UC Berkeley and is scientifically proven to inspire awe.

1 Think back to a time when you experienced awe and write about it in as much detail as possible. Make it so vivid that a director could make a movie scene from your description.

2 After writing, take a deep breath, and complete this sentence stem: "Right now I feel _____ ."

CHAPTER

13

self-love   and   confidence

If you've read any part of this book, it's no secret that one of my greatest challenges in this life has been growing into my self-love and confidence. When I first moved to LA for college, I developed a pretty severe eating disorder. This is more common than you would imagine in men, yet it's rarely discussed. I even created a music video about it called "Broken Mirrors." Back then, I was trying to make myself perfect—to fit the impossible standard of male beauty, thinking if I had zero percent body fat and an eight pack of abs, then I would finally be loved and validated. One of my lowest moments came when I was nineteen. I had just forced myself to throw up again. But this time was different. I walked over to the sink, looked into the mirror, and all I saw was red. Blood. Gushing inside my eyeball. This time I had gone too far. The pressure of throwing up had popped a blood vessel in my eye.

I've come a long way from that day when I was nineteen, struggling with an eating disorder, pretending I had it all together, when really I was a mess inside. Healing from that level of self-hatred was one of the greatest challenges of my life, but it also provided some of my greatest gifts and lessons. And in this chapter I'm passing those lessons on to you. I know what it feels like to hold up a façade of perfection. I know what it's like to always worry about what other people think. I know what it's like to always be comparing yourself to others. I created the guided minipractices in this chapter to help you remember that you are worthy just as you are.

FORGIVING YOURSELF

"Show me the lesson."

We all have moments when we look back upon the successes of the past, striving to return to a moment that is gone. We look at old photos of our young bodies, reminisce about the old days of new love, and fanaticize about reigniting a flame that has long since burned out. There is beauty in cherishing your journey, but trying to recreate the past only sparks an endless cycle of pain that will blind you from new possibilities.

If you constantly compare yourself to who you were in the past, it becomes impossible to make magic with the life you have right now.

Give yourself permission to change. It's okay to slow down. It's okay to rest.

Forgive yourself for not living up to your own expectations.
Forgive yourself for letting yourself go sometimes.
Forgive yourself for falling off track.
Forgive yourself for not always having the perfect body,
for not always accomplishing everything on time,
for not always listening to your intuition.
Forgive yourself.

Every time you fall off track, you are just being polished and refined to become that much stronger, smarter, and wiser.

Let go of what was. Release your guilt. Forgive yourself. Then find your new center—with compassion.[1]

The Practice

Close your eyes, place your hands over your heart, and initiate your Freedom Meditation practice by whispering the anchor mantra "Show me the lesson." Whisper it to yourself tenderly. Trust in the universe. There are no mistakes. You are exactly where you are supposed to be right now.

If you prefer to be guided through the audio version of this experience, go to justinmichaelwilliams.com/staywoke.

JOURNAL PROMPTS

1 What do you need to forgive yourself for?

2 What caused you to fall off track? And what valuable lesson did you learn from taking that detour?

3 Given the new perspective you have now, what do you want to change about your life and vision moving forward?

4 What's the first step of your new journey?

IF YOU CONSTANTLY COMPARE YOURSELF TO WHO YOU WERE IN THE PAST, IT BECOMES IMPOSSIBLE TO MAKE MAGIC WITH THE LIFE YOU HAVE RIGHT NOW.

THE PRISON OF PERFECTIONISM

ANCHOR MANTRA

"I am worthy as I am, right now."

In 2018, I was at the Wanderlust conference listening to my soul sister, wellness disruptive, and social activist Kerri Kelly, give a talk about overcoming perfection. She said something that pierced right through to the core of my being: "Perfectionism is oppression. It's a system that profits on our 'not enoughness.' And it has one purpose—to maintain control and power."[2]

They tell us, "Buy this and you will be happy. Eat that and you will be healthy. Read this and you will be enlightened. Take that class, lose more weight, apply more contour, get that degree, make more money, buy that house, keep feeding the system—then you'll finally be ready for (and worthy of) your dream."

Perfectionism fools us into prioritizing acceptance and validation over our purpose and calling. It gives us the illusion that we are in control, when really we are just spellbound by our fear.

How many songs, stories, scripts, business ideas, relationships, and dreams have you buried, waiting for the impossibility of perfection to let them bloom?

Read this carefully: **You do not need to be perfect to be deserving of the things you really want in your life**. You are whole in your imperfection, exactly as you are right now.

Move forward in spite of your fear. Tell those voices screaming for perfection to STFU. Then prove them wrong. That's how we take back control. That's how we break the system. The time is now.

The Practice

Start your practice with the STFU Breath. Inhale for 6 counts and then exhale for as long as possible (try for 20–30 seconds), making a long "shhhhhh" sound, like you're telling someone to be quiet. Repeat three times.

Then place your hands over your naval, take several deep breaths, and introduce the anchor mantra "I am worthy as I am, right now" into your Freedom Meditation practice.

If you prefer to be guided through the audio version of this experience, go to justinmichaelwilliams.com/staywoke.

JOURNAL PROMPTS

1 In what area of your life are you paralyzed by perfectionism? Hint: if you've been working on something but continue to tweak, tweak, and tweak the idea into a grave of exhaustion, you are under the spell of perfectionism.

2 What is one step you could take to move the idea forward in spite of your fear? Done is better than perfect.

YOU DO NOT NEED TO BE PERFECT TO BE DESERVING OF THE THINGS YOU REALLY WANT IN YOUR LIFE.

STOP BEING SO HARD ON YOURSELF

ANCHOR MANTRA

"I trust, I let go."

All of our lives are a mess sometimes. Yes, even mine. You see the smile, the book, the podcasts, the album, and the articles talking about my success. But what you don't see are the thousands of times I've been told no, only to get that one yes I posted about online. You don't see me crumpled in tears on the floor from yet another lover who says, "You chose work over the relationship." You don't see me gripping my lower belly in the mirror, trying to hold back the echoes of my college eating disorder.

We all have highs and lows. We all find ourselves in unimaginable situations. We all feel lost, confused, and hopeless sometimes. Life can be messy. And I think more of us need to be honest about that. Social media will have you believe other people are out there living these perfect, easy, lavish lives, but **you can't compare yourself to other people—you don't know what they sacrificed to get there**.

I'm going to let you in on a little secret: "having it all" doesn't make you happy. "Knowing your purpose" doesn't make you happy. "Success" doesn't make you happy. *Connection* is what makes you happy—connection to Self, to others, and to something greater.

So the next time you're feeling alone, depressed, sad, or like you don't have it all figured out . . . relax. If it's really *for you*, it will happen. You don't have to try so hard. You don't have to force it. You don't have to be so hard on yourself. We're all just figuring this shit out. And we're all in this thing together.

YOU CAN'T COMPARE YOURSELF TO OTHER PEOPLE— YOU DON'T KNOW WHAT THEY SACRIFICED TO GET THERE.

The Practice

Close your eyes, place your hands over your heart, and take eight deep breaths, inhaling through the nose and exhaling through the mouth. Begin your Freedom Meditation practice using the anchor mantra "I trust, I let go."

Trust there is a power greater than you at work here. Surrender to it. Rest in it. You are exactly where you are supposed to be, even if you don't understand it now. Trust.

If you prefer to be guided through the audio version of this experience, go to justinmichaelwilliams.com/staywoke.

JOURNAL PROMPTS

Next time you're being hard on yourself, close your eyes, take five deep breaths, and complete these sentence stems:

"Right now I feel _____ ."

"And I hate this feeling because _____ _____ ."

"And if I allowed this feeling to scream, it would say _ _____ ."

"What would soothe me most right now is _____ ."

"A way I can give that to myself is _ _____ ."

Now go do it.

If I could write a love letter to my younger self,
knowing everything I know now, it would say something like this.

Dear beautiful Justin,

Embrace your weirdness, baby. Because the things that make you different are the things that make you fucking MAGICAL.

All the things you're ashamed of are the very things you're going to be celebrated for when you get older.

Sure, your voice is a little high and squeaky—but that voice is going to inspire millions.

And yes, you got a little shuga in ya tank—but boy, you can work a stage like no other.

So stop trying to fit in.

The sooner you come to love and accept your random quirks, the sooner your life will transform into something more magical than you could've ever dreamed of.

I love you.

P.S. All the people who are teasing you about being gay, well . . . they're gay, too; they're just hurting.

I joined forces with my dear friend Jay R. Cambridge, founder of Live Outside the Box, to create a special practice for you. Jay is a transgender military veteran who used to struggle with anxiety and fear of being different. But yoga changed all that. This quote of his says it all: "When I finally took the time to just be still, and be with myself; to reflect inward, and really get to know myself, my values, and what mattered to me in this life—that's when things started to change."[3]

The following practice was designed to help you in moments when you feel like you don't belong, when you're worried about what other people think, or when you simply need a confidence boost.

The Practice

Stand in the mirror and look yourself directly in the eyes. Stand as close to the mirror as you can, until your lips are almost touching it. Place a hand over your heart, look into your right eye, and say these words ten times: "[Insert your name], you are so fucking magical." Then do it again ten times while looking into your left eye. As I mentioned in chapter 3, affirmations are more of a Band-Aid than a permanent fix; they won't get rid of the source of your problems, but a good pep talk might get you into a more positive headspace to do the deeper work.

After your mirror work, immediately close your eyes and drop into your Freedom Meditation practice, using Jay's inspiring slogan as your anchor mantra: "Be you. Be true. That's beautiful."

If you prefer to be guided through the audio version of this experience, go to justinmichaelwilliams.com/staywoke.

JOURNAL PROMPTS

1 Write a love note to your childhood self. Knowing what you know now, what would you say to the younger you?

2 Now that you've elevated your vibration, go back to chapter 3 and do the Toxic Thoughts: Stopping Self-Criticism guided practice again. This time, use your current toxic thoughts and self-judgments as the focus.

GOT OVERACHIEVERS' SYNDROME? THIS WILL HELP

ANCHOR MANTRA

"Who I am matters more."

If you're always busy, overcommitted, stretched too thin, overworked, overfunctioning, and generally overachieving, then you're probably infected with Overachievers' Syndrome. The most common symptom is fooling yourself into thinking it's all for "success." But we all know that's not the case. If hard work were equated to success, then everyone working sixty hours a week would be rich and happy.

I believe what we really want is to know that *we are enough*.

Yet somehow, when we were younger, most of us got fooled into thinking that if we achieve enough, work enough, accomplish enough, and do enough, we will finally *be enough*. But this is a vicious cycle—a classic type-A dysfunction that leads down a lonely road on the never-ending pursuit of purpose. This is the lesson that took me the longest to learn. And as somebody who is in recovery from Overachievers' Syndrome, I want you to know that you are enough, as you are, right now. Just for being you.

You are more than your successes.

You are more than your accomplishments.

You are more than the money you have in the bank.

Who you are matters more.

It's time to prioritize your spirit over success.

The Practice

Try to stop being so hard on yourself. It doesn't become you.

Close your eyes, place your hands over your heart, and take five deep breaths. Initiate your Freedom Meditation practice using the anchor mantra "Who I am matters more."

If you prefer to be guided through the audio version of this experience, go to justinmichaelwilliams.com/staywoke.

JOURNAL PROMPTS

1 Why are you working yourself so hard? Go deep: what is the *real* reason?
2 When did you get the idea that hard work equals success? Has it proven to be true? Is that *really* working for you?
3 What are the costs of working yourself so hard? Are you losing sleep? Destroying relationships? Missing important moments with family?
4 What qualities do you value most in others? What qualities do you value most in yourself? Write down 5 *qualities of character* that have nothing to do with achievement or success.

GET BETTER AT SAYING, "NO!"

ANCHOR MANTRA

"I don't have to be afraid. I'm allowed to say no."

How many times have you said yes to someone and immediately felt regret afterward?

"Yes, I'll listen to you talk about your [*same damn problems over and over*]."

"Yes, I'll meet you for coffee so you can pick my brain [*even though you should be paying me for it*]."

"Yes, I'll go on a date with you [*even though I really don't even like you*]."

Every time you say yes when you really want to say no, you contaminate your relationships with resentment, with the feeling that the other person is "forcing" you to do something, when, in fact, *you* were the one with the porous boundaries.

It seems counterintuitive at first, but saying no protects your relationships, because you'll avoid growing an underlying seed of resentment for all the times you've said yes and didn't mean it.

Give yourself permission to say no.

Give yourself permission to say, "Let me think about it and get back to you."

Saying yes when you don't mean it is an assault on your intuition—and it will slowly ruin all of your relationships.

The Practice

Use this practice anytime you're having trouble saying no.

Place your hands over your heart, take five deep breaths, and initiate your Freedom Meditation practice using the anchor mantra "I don't have to be afraid. I'm allowed to say no."

If you prefer to be guided through the audio version of this experience, go to justinmichaelwilliams.com/staywoke.

JOURNAL PROMPTS

1 How does it feel if you say yes to someone when you really wanted to say no? Do you feel anything in your body? In your mind? In your emotional field?
2 What is driving you to say yes in those instances?
3 What are you afraid will happen if you say no?
4 By saying no, what can you do with your time instead?
5 What's one thing you can remind yourself of next time you're afraid to say no?

SAYING YES WHEN YOU DON'T MEAN IT IS AN ASSAULT ON YOUR INTUITION— AND IT WILL SLOWLY RUIN ALL OF YOUR RELATIONSHIPS.

FIVE SELF-CARE HACKS FOR BUSY MOMS AND DADS

ANCHOR MANTRA

"By loving me, I'm loving you."

My mom, Barbara, is Supermom. Looking back, I really don't know how she did it all. She worked a full-time job, yet still managed to cook dinner (almost) every night and take care of three kids mostly on her own. She was at every school meeting, every big performance, and every sports game, cheering me on from the sidelines. My mom will always be my biggest fan, and for that, I am forever grateful.

But sometimes I feel bad for her. She gave up everything for us—her passions, her hobbies, but most significantly, her self-care.

I'm not a parent, and I hate when people who don't have lived experience try to give me advice, so I interviewed Erin Falconer, author of *How To Get Sh*t Done: Why Women Need to Stop Doing Everything So They Can Achieve Anything*, to see what advice she could offer to help you up-level your self-care game.[4] Erin is a mom, a successful entrepreneur, and a committed meditator. Her practical tips will help parents of all kinds—especially if your house is noisy, your time is limited, and you're often stretched too thin.

IF YOU DON'T TAKE CARE OF YOURSELF AND YOU DON'T TAKE CARE OF YOUR RELATIONSHIP, WHAT YOU'RE CREATING FOR YOUR CHILD, FROM DAY ONE, IS A BROKEN HOME.

1 **Reorder your priorities**. It might feel counterintuitive at first, but experts say your order of priorities should be as follows:

- Most important: the relationship you have with yourself
- Second: the relationship you have with your partner
- Third: the relationship you have with your child

If you don't take care of yourself and you don't take care of your relationship, what you're creating for your child, from day one, is a broken home. And what's the best thing you can do for any child? Create a rock-solid home. You can't do that when you've thrown yourself and your relationship under the bus. So even though instinctually you want to be available 24/7 and give every ounce of energy to your kid, don't. That's a short-term solution and unsustainable. When you're raising a child, you have to think long term—and that means creating a stable, loving environment. By spending time on you and your relationship, you are tilling fertile soil in which your child can bloom.

2 **Make the bathroom your sanctuary**. Having ten minutes to wash your face and brush your teeth without interruption can be a blessing when you're a new parent, so indulge in the bathroom intentionally. Steam up the shower, sit on the floor and meditate, or even just take an extra two minutes on the toilet to sit still and breathe. Pro tip: Keep a scented candle in your bathroom and light it only during your "me time." This will become a sacred ritual to help you relax and center your mind.

3 **Create a daily anchor**. You don't need hours of free time to practice self-care—all you need is a ten- to twenty-minute anchor every day. Most of us use our free time to talk on the phone, scroll though social media, or catch up with friends. Don't. You need that time as a reprieve from the rocky waters of parenthood—to restore your balance, process your emotions, and evaluate what's happening in your life. Once you create a rhythm with your daily anchor, everything else will start to fall into place.

4 **Make afternoons your mornings.** Morning routines aren't realistic for all parents, especially working ones, so use the afternoon instead. Everyone with a job has a lunch break; make yours special. Eat your lunch quickly, then go to your car, an empty office, or a quiet space near your building to practice your daily self-care ritual. On days when you're feeling depleted, this will renew your energy.

5 **Be intentional about your "me time."** How you approach your "me time" matters. Make every second of it count. Even if you only have seven minutes, set an alarm and use it to relax (instead of micromanaging, worrying, and planning). Seven minutes can be completely rejuvenating when you're running on fumes. Be grateful for the time you have, instead of thinking of it as being too short.

I'll close with my favorite quote from my conversation with Erin: "I think there's a lot of guilt associated with parenting. It's like if we're not spending every second with our kids, we think they're going to feel abandoned or something. But what I've learned is that it's *not* about time; *it's about the energy you bring.* I would rather see my kid for just a few hours a day when I am present and full of energy than seeing him eight hours a day while I'm exhausted, irritable, and moody. We have to change our perspective. It's not about the time you're giving, it's about the quality of energy you can bring to your child in whatever time you have."[5]

Your kids are going to remember the fun times you shared together, but they'll also remember the negative moments—the times you yelled at them because you were stressed, and the times when you snapped at your partner because you were sleep deprived.

The following practice and journal prompts were created to help you relax in your "me time" so that you can nourish yourself and create a safe, loving, and secure home for your family.

The Practice

Start your practice using the 6 Count Breath: inhale for 6 counts, hold for 6 counts, exhale for 6 counts. Repeat 3 times. Then initiate your Freedom Meditation practice using the anchor mantra "By loving me, I'm loving you."

Try to be intentional about this moment. Don't use it to worry or plan.

If you prefer to be guided through the audio version of this experience, go to justinmichaelwilliams.com/staywoke.

JOURNAL PROMPTS

1 The recipe for a tense home environment is an exhausted and depleted parent. What can you do today to take care of you? How does taking this time contribute to the health of your home?

2 A broken home isn't just defined by a single-parent household. If your home is full of tension, your child will feel it. If you have a partner, what can you do today to nourish your relationship with them? How can you respect your partner more (even when you're moody)? If you don't have a partner, write about someone else in your life whom you have tension with (for example, your parents, grandparents, or close friends).

3 Write down five easy things you can do to practice self-care. Keep this list in your phone so you can remember to use it when you have a few minutes to spare.

Several years ago, I was leading a meditation workshop of about thirty-five people, and we got to the point in class when I ask everyone to create their mantra and share it with the group. As usual, we went around the circle, sharing one by one, in deep reverence for each person's unique offering. People were saying beautiful things like "love," "inner peace," "power," and "confidence." And then we got to a young black boy named Galen. He paused for an awkwardly long period of time, closed his eyes, and finally said with confidence, "I am Beyoncé."

You should've seen the look on everyone's faces. The rest of the students were holding back giggles, waiting to see if I would make a correction . . . but I understood him.

I will never forget my first Beyoncé concert. It was Monday, July 13, 2009, at the STAPLES Center in Los Angeles. I had been to many concerts in my life, but what Beyoncé did that night ignited something in me that I didn't know was possible. For the first time ever, I saw what true mastery looked like. I spent most of the show watching Beyoncé in a state of pure awe—jaw dropped to the floor, blown back into my seat, and on the verge of tears all night long. But every few moments, I would sneak and turn toward the audience, imagining what it would be like *if I were the one on that stage*. How would it feel to *be* Beyoncé?

To many of us, Beyoncé represents the most awakened version of Self: anything is possible, no challenge too big to surmount, no dream too wild to pursue. Beyoncé represents life at its prime, all the time. Healed. No chains. Queen. Royalty.

But what I want you to remember is that it's all a projection. Everything Beyoncé represents is already inside each of us.

The following practice will help you get into formation—to awaken your power, presence, mastery, and greatness, inspired by one of the greatest artists of all time.

The Practice

Start by watching a video of one of your favorite Beyoncé performances. My favorites:

- "Sweet Dreams Medley (Wynn Las Vegas)"
- "Super Bowl 2013 Halftime Show"
- "Freedom (BET Awards 2016)"

Then immediately dive into your Freedom Meditation practice, using all that emotion and inspiration you feel. Use the anchor mantra "I am power. I am greatness."

If you prefer to be guided through the audio version of this experience, go to justinmichaelwilliams.com/staywoke.

JOURNAL PROMPTS

1 Beyoncé is a reflection, a mirror of your inherent greatness. What qualities do you see in Beyoncé that you want to activate within yourself?

2 How do you feel watching her performances? What emotions get charged up inside of you?

3 What other things in your life activate that same type of energy? Is it your job, a social justice movement, a passion project, a relationship?

4 How can you commit to spending more quality time engaging in the activity you identified in the previous question? This will be a source of power for you.

CHAPTER

14

Your instincts are throwing up a red flag. You're stressed and anxious, so you call your friends to ask for advice, but none of it seems quite right.

"I don't know if I can trust him."

"I don't know if I can trust her."

"I'm not sure if I should trust this situation."

But the truth is, you don't need to trust anybody else—you need to learn to trust yourself.

Trusting yourself means having the courage to *show up, make a change, or get out* when a situation arises that's not serving your highest good. If you promise always to trust your intuition, then you never have to worry about making "wrong" choices, because you know every situation is here to teach you something. And if you get off track, you just have to course correct. But to *trust* your intuition, first you have to be able to *access* your intuition.

The guided practices in this chapter have three goals:

1 To bring you into greater internal alignment so you can access your intuition

2 To remove the cloudiness and static that keep you lost in uncertainty

3 To sharpen your focus so you can get sh!t done

The worst place to be is stuck. It's time to make a move. You're going to learn lessons either way.

THE WORST PLACE TO BE IS STUCK.
IT'S TIME TO MAKE A MOVE. YOU'RE GOING
TO LEARN LESSONS EITHER WAY.

AM I IN THE WRONG RELATIONSHIP?

ANCHOR MANTRA

"If I really believed I was worthy, what would I do?"

My darling, you are worth so much more than this. I know it seems impossible right now. I know it seems scary. I know you've become so entangled that you don't see a way through. I know you're trying to be optimistic and imagine the best possible outcome. But it's not your job to fix everything.

My darling, I know you always see the best in people, but please don't let this steal your shine. The world needs your shine. Your family needs your shine. Your community needs your shine. Don't give it to someone who doesn't deserve it.

My darling, what is it about your worth that you lift people up at the expense of your own light?

I need you to know this: **everything you are waiting for is on the other side of that change.**

It's time.

You don't have to be afraid.

You already know the answer.

Trust yourself.

The Practice

Close your eyes, place your hands over your heart, and repeat the STFU Breath three times to start your practice. Inhale for 6 counts and exhale while making a long "shhhhhh" sound, like you're telling someone to be quiet. Try to make your exhales at least 20—30 seconds long.

Now drop into your Freedom Meditation practice using the anchor mantra "If I really believed I was worthy, what would I do?" Trust what arises.

If you prefer to be guided through the audio version of this experience, go to justinmichaelwilliams.com/staywoke.

JOURNAL PROMPTS

1 What is your instinct telling you to do?

2 What are you afraid will happen if you follow it?

3 Can you think of a time when you trusted your instinct before and it turned out well? Write about it.

4 What if you made the change and everything worked out better than you expected? How would that look? Describe it.

5 What's the next best move?

WHAT IS IT ABOUT YOUR WORTH THAT YOU LIFT PEOPLE UP AT THE EXPENSE OF YOUR OWN LIGHT?

DUI CHECKPOINT: ARE YOUR VICES HOLDING YOU BACK?

ANCHOR MANTRA

"Where am I out of alignment?" or "I am all that I need."

Dreaming Under the Influence (DUI) (*verb*): the attempt to manifest with an impaired connection to Spirit.

When I was preparing to write my album, my dear friend and spiritual mentor Brenda Villa told me that I needed to stop drinking alcohol. Not because I had an addiction problem, but because drinking made me cloudy, and I could not afford to be cloudy at such a pivotal moment in my life. She said, "There's a reason women don't drink when they're pregnant. And right now you are giving birth to an entirely new life."

The twenty-six-year-old version of me who enjoyed an occasional cocktail didn't want to admit it, but I knew Brenda was right. Alcohol was creating static in my connection to Spirit.

Most of us think our vices give us energy—that they make us more creative, more social, more sexual, and more free. But the truth is, your vices don't *give* you anything—they just temporarily numb the layers of shame, guilt, and trauma that cause you to hold yourself back in the first place.

I started numbing at a very young age. I smoked weed and drank alcohol for the first time when I was fourteen, and I started using cocaine, Adderall, ecstasy, and mushrooms when I was in college. So trust me—when I'm talking about numbing your pain through drugs, I'm speaking from experience. Although I do believe there are some environments where substances can be healing, most of us don't use them that way. The purpose of this practice is not to lecture you about partying or to promote complete sobriety—there are no judgments here. This is simply an invitation to prioritize your connection to Spirit.

Who are you underneath all of your vices?

Who are you underneath the caffeine that makes you a chronic overfunctioner, the weed that makes you "more creative," and the alcohol that makes you "have more fun" in environments where you'd usually be bored out of your mind?

Who would you be without a stimulant to make you more or a suppressant to make you less? **And what if that version of you was enough?**

Underneath all those vices, there is a light, there is a power, there is a radiance that the world deserves to see and you deserve to know. But most of all, there is clarity.

And my hope is that you get to experience it, because it is from that place that your life transforms most quickly.

The Practice

Place your hands over your heart and drop the first suggested anchor mantra, "Where am I out of alignment?," into your Freedom Meditation practice. Whisper it to yourself and be open to the answers that come.

Once you identify a vice that is pulling you out of alignment, consider releasing it for a specific number of days, like we discussed in chapter 3 about toxic habits.

If you've already given up a vice and need a tool to keep you on track, use this anchor mantra instead: "I am all that I need."

If you prefer to be guided through the audio version of this experience, go to justinmichaelwilliams.com/staywoke.

JOURNAL PROMPTS

1 What causes you to reach for one of your vices?
2 What feeling are you trying to avoid by using this vice?
3 What energy are you trying to activate by using this vice? For example, does it make you more social? Less anxious? More creative? More sexual?
4 How would your life transform if you could activate that energy on your own, without using the vice?
5 Are you willing to experiment with giving up this vice? If so, for how long?

Weed might help you get you out of your head, make you more comfortable around people, soothe your anxiety, help you focus, make you more creative, calm down all the noise in your mind, eliminate all your negative thoughts—hell, sometimes weed might even make you feel like you're "the shit." I get it.

But what if weed doesn't do any of that?

What if it's just waking up an energy that's already inside of you? And what if you could get a hit of that magic without smoking at all?

You can do this with meditation.

In nearly every class I teach, someone always sheepishly says, "I've been thinking, like . . . *maybe I smoke too much*?" People *know* when they have a borderline toxic relationship with weed—their intuition has been whispering it to them all along—but they're afraid to admit it because "everybody does it," so how could it be bad for you? Right?

I don't believe weed is inherently toxic, and I do believe it can be used for healing. But for most of us, weed can become a crutch. How amazing would it be if you didn't need to rely on something external to make you feel okay inside? Underneath the haze of all that smoke, there's a natural wellspring of charisma, creativity, and productivity that's more powerful than you could ever imagine.

This practice will help you unblock it.

The Practice

I recommend using the guided audio version of this practice from my website to immerse yourself fully in the experience. You can also use the instructions below.

First, answer this question: "WHAT is it that you're taking a hit of?" Meaning, what energy does weed provide for you? Is it confidence? Creativity? Relaxation? You decide. **Your answer will be your unique anchor mantra for this practice.**

Then, visualize yourself being immersed in a room filled with smoke from the bombest California weed; it's the highest quality weed you've ever had. Imagine the smoke filling the room, surrounding you like in a hotbox, but without any of the coughing. It's perfect. It's like weed heaven. Picture it as vividly as possible. You might see an image, smell it, taste it, hear sounds, feel sensations, or experience a change in emotions.

Once you feel immersed, start to deepen your breath.

On each inhale, imagine the smoke entering your body the same way it does when you take a hit—but this smoke penetrates deeper. Hold your breath for a moment, like you were savoring the most delicately rolled joint. And then let it out slowly. Every time you inhale, imagine the smoke filling every crevice of your inner body, healing any part of you that needs some extra love. This sacred smoke is like sage, clearing your energy field. Immerse yourself in it.

Continue breathing deeply for 3—5 minutes. Every breath is an opportunity to get a hit of exactly what you need. Don't be afraid to make a little noise while you do this. Pretend you are actually smoking your mantra.

If you prefer to be guided through the audio version of this experience, go to justinmichaelwilliams.com/staywoke.

JOURNAL PROMPTS

1 Take five deep breaths and complete this sentence stem: "If I don't smoke weed, I'm afraid I won't be _____ enough."
2 What uncomfortable emotion are you trying to cover up when you smoke?
3 What aspect of your personality are you trying to enhance when you smoke?
4 How would you use weed differently if you believed your natural energy was *enough*?
5 What's one baby step you could take toward shifting your relationship with weed? Think of it like an experiment: judgment free, all about learning.

STOP PORN FROM F*CKING YOU: A CREATIVITY PRACTICE

ANCHOR MANTRA

"Use me, creativity. I am yours."

Picture this.

It's 3:00 a.m. on a Wednesday night, and I'm wide awake in bed. It's pitch-black in my room other than a soft blue glow from my computer screen. I had promised myself I would go to bed early because I need to wake up at 8:00 a.m., and I did . . . I got in bed at 11:00 p.m., for God's sake, but I made one time-sucking mistake: watching porn. And four hours later, I'm still there, hypnotized, scrolling past page 82 of the "Ebony" section of Pornhub, trying to find the perfect camera angle to get me off so that I can soothe my anxiety and finally go to sleep. "It was supposed to be quick," I'm thinking, "but none of my favorite videos seem to be doing the trick. I miss Tumblr. Maybe I'll try Xtube. Or maybe I should download Grindr again? Ugh . . . it's getting late. I better just get this over with."

[Cue wave of extreme guilt.]

"Four hours, Justin? Really? Think of how much work you could've done in FOUR FREAKIN' HOURS! Ugh. I better go pee and then get my ass to bed—I gotta wake up soon."

Sound familiar? If so, you definitely want to keep reading.

One of the most life-altering positive changes I've made in the last several years was shifting my relationship to porn.

Now, I don't want to create a judgmental, binary narrative about porn being "bad," because it's not that simple. I do, however, want to educate you with some of the science and teach you a mindfulness technique that can help you overcome your addiction to porn so that your:

- Relationships can get better
- Sex life can improve
- Creativity can blossom
- Anxiety can decrease
- Sleep patterns can get better

And yes, porn does affect *all* that stuff.

Porn is like an addictive drug: it floods your brain with high levels of dopamine. The more you watch, the more dopamine you get, and the stronger and more uncontrollable your cravings become—which is how one "quick hit" turns into four hours of lost sleep.[1]

Science has proven that watching too much porn causes:

- Less sexual satisfaction within a relationship
- Difficulty getting aroused by the same partner
- Low sex drive, erectile dysfunction, trouble reaching an orgasm
- Loneliness, anxiety, depression, self-loathing
- Increased risk of infidelity
- Greater likelihood for divorce
- Skewed and unhealthy views about sex[2]

And for men: constant ejaculation also affects your creativity. Sexuality is directly linked to creative energy. So every time you release, you have to rebuild. But most of us are releasing so often that we never give our creativity time to fully recharge. Imagine how much more powerful you would be if you had access to *all* of your creative energy. Don't worry, I'm not suggesting that you become chaste or join the convent. Being horny or turned on is not bad or unspiritual. But consider that you can harness and redirect your sexual energy for more than just a fleeting moment of pleasure.

If you're still with me, this practice will help.

The Practice

Set your intention on something you are creating—your art, business, relationship, et cetera.

Find a comfortable seat, close your eyes, and start squeezing your pelvic floor in a slow pulsing rhythm, using the same muscles you would squeeze while holding your pee. Don't squeeze too tight—just imagine you're squeezing a ripe plum. You should feel a tingling sensation in your genitals. Continue the squeezing and releasing for 30 seconds to 2 minutes.

After you begin to tingle down there, start your Freedom Meditation practice using the anchor mantra "Use me, creativity. I am yours."

I use this practice before I go on stage, before I write, or before any creative session. Even a two-minute practice will boost your creative energy, and the best part is, no one can tell that you're doing it, so squeeze away!

If you prefer to be guided through the audio version of this experience, go to justinmichaelwilliams.com/staywoke.

JOURNAL PROMPTS

1 What's your relationship with porn? Be honest. No one's reading . . .

2 What usually triggers you to go on a porn binge? Boredom? Anxiety? Stress? Loneliness? If you don't know, track it next time.

3 Could you use your creative energy for something else instead of watching porn? A passion project? A relationship? How could you harness that energy for something more meaningful?

4 Next time you get stuck in a porn loop, what is one thing you can say to yourself to remind you to use your energy differently?

When your mom gets a message from your third-grade teacher at noon saying, "Call back immediately," it's never good news. Earlier that morning, my teacher had given our class an assignment to draw a picture of our "perfect world." So I grabbed the best colors from my 256 pack of Crayola crayons, pulled out my favorite scented markers, and got to work. When it was time to share, all of my classmates held up pictures of rainbows, butterflies, and people holding hands. Then it was my turn. I held up my masterpiece—a picture of a huge glass bubble. Inside the bubble was fake grass, electronic dogs and cats, "no bugs," "no trees," and oxygen getting pumped in from tanks so that "no one ever had allergies." On the top of the page, I drew big red block letters that read, "I HATE NATURE."

Kids who grow up in inner-city communities are often stripped of the experience of nature. Allergy pills and asthma inhalers are used like shields to protect us from an environment most of our parents consider the Unknown. We are taught to be afraid of being outside. Hell, imagine what could happen to a young black boy wearing a hoodie alone in the woods at night? That's where the lynchings happen, that's where the crosses get burned, that's where you get dragged from the back of a pickup truck by the KKK.

Those were the images of nature ingrained in my mind as a kid: all fear.

Whether you grew up in the hood or not, we all need to spend more time outside. Being in nature is scientifically proven to reduce stress and anxiety, relieve obsessive thinking, increase your attention span, boost your creativity *and* productivity, and inspire you to be more kind and generous.[3] Being in nature also affects your physical health; recent studies are proving that being exposed to nature even helps you recover from illnesses faster.[4]

Although scientists can prove that nature heals, they can't yet figure out *why*. I believe it's because by connecting with nature, we are connecting to one of our greatest sources of communal power. Nature is the one place we can all go—beyond race, beyond gender, beyond religion, beyond creed—to connect. If you want to see how to do something right, just watch nature. She doesn't discriminate; she supports all of us; and she lets everything die when its time comes, knowing that nothing is ever lost. Nature is our greatest teacher. Nature is God manifest. And we *are* nature.

In my early twenties, my dear friend Sianna Sherman, visionary and founder of Rasa Yoga, took me under her wing and taught me how to connect with nature for the first time. I'll warn you now, you're going to feel weird AF doing these things at first, but trust me, they work.

Here are five ways to deepen your connection with nature:

1. **Find a special tree that you can visit regularly.** It can be in your yard, in your neighborhood, or even on a hike. Anytime you're going through a challenge, stand or sit with your back up against your special tree, close your eyes, and let its wisdom speak to you.

2. **Write a secret song or poem for nature.** Think of it like a secret handshake— don't share it with anyone else.

3. **Bring gifts.** Every time I go on a hike, I bring some crumbs of food to leave with the trees and plants. This is a sacred offering—a gift of thanks for the wisdom and beauty nature blesses us with every day. Leaving food also brings more life to the plants and trees.

4. **Buy a plant and name it.** You don't have to live near an oasis to connect with nature. Buy a plant for your home, name it, talk to it, meditate with it, and build a relationship with it. A plant isn't just another piece of furniture; it's a living being that is literally making oxygen for your home.

5. **Leave your gadgets behind.** If you use your brain to multitask all day (like most of us do), leave your tech behind and go on a five- to ten-minute walk around your neighborhood, paying special attention to all the nature you encounter. Science proves that it doesn't take hours of free time for nature to impact your wellbeing— within just five minutes, your brain starts to change. So go walk around your block! This practice gives your prefrontal cortex time to recover, which inspires bursts of creativity, stimulates problem solving, and boosts your mood.[5]

In an era when we spend more and more time online, we must make nature a priority. The invisible energy that makes your heart beat without you ever thinking about it is the same energy that makes the world spin and the waves slap against the shore. Nature is inside each of us. We must protect her, we must love her, and we must accept her invitation to connect.

The following practice was designed to help you connect deeply with the wisdom of nature.

The Practice

Sit with your back up against a tree, lie in the grass, or just stand outside with your shoes off. Close your eyes and begin to breathe deeply. On each inhale, imagine breathing in the energy, wisdom, and protection of the earth. Relax into it. Let nature's healing bathe every inch of your body. On each exhale, send any heavy, stagnant energy down into the earth. Let it transmute and drain from your system. Continue this breathing and releasing process for as long as you need, until you feel renewed. You can be greedy about it; Mother Nature has enough energy to go around.

Then begin your Freedom Meditation practice, using the anchor mantra "What do I need to know?" And let the wisdom of nature speak to you.

> If you prefer to be guided through the audio version of this experience, go to justinmichaelwilliams.com/staywoke.

JOURNAL PROMPTS

1 What's an easy way that you can be in nature more frequently? Even a few minutes makes a difference.

2 Have you ever experienced any wisdom messages or creative downloads from nature? If so, write a quick thank-you note.

3 Do you have any fears or hesitations about being in nature? If so, what are they? Where did they come from? Are they true?

Have you ever woken up in the morning, scrolled through your phone, seen a post about something terrible that happened in the world, and then been unable to stop thinking about it all day? Do you ever have days where you feel a little gloomy or depressed but can't figure out why?

Oftentimes, the culprit is your morning routine.

When you first wake up, your brain is in a similar state to that of hypnosis— highly suggestible—so what you do, think, and consume during this time influences the rest of your day.

The following minipractices should be done within the first fifteen minutes of your day to supplement your Daily Meditation Ritual. Some of these practices take only one or two minutes. I'm not asking you to wake up extra early or make a dramatic change in your life. Just experiment to see what works best for you.

Here are five ways to get inspired every morning (without waking up early!):

1   **Take five deep breaths and set an intention for your day.** Immediately after waking up, lie in bed and take five purposeful, slow, deep breaths. Inhale through your nose and exhale through your mouth. Then set an intention for the energy you'd like to cultivate throughout your day.

2   **Do a quick gratitude practice.** Keep a small gratitude journal next to your bed. After your alarm rings, reach over and write down three things you have to be grateful for. This is scientifically proven to cultivate happiness. I detailed how to build a gratitude practice and all the benefits in chapter 12.

3   **Listen to an inspirational podcast.** Instead of scrolling through your news feed, start your day with an inspirational podcast. Some of my favorites: *Motivation for Black People* (shameless plug), *Oprah's SuperSoul Conversations*, *SoulFeed*, and *Pick the Brain*. It's easy to listen on your phone while you're showering, getting dressed, or in the car, so this is a great option if you're always running behind schedule.

4   **Read a poem, quote, or short passage from a book.** One of my clients had an idea to create a "quote jar"—a mason jar she filled with her favorite motivational quotes and memes. Every morning she picks one out to set the

tone for her day. You can also read a passage from a spiritual text or from my personal favorites—Oprah's *Wisdom of Sundays* book or *The Radiance Sutras* by Lorin Roche.

5 **Pull a tarot card.** After your morning meditation, try pulling a tarot card to receive your intuitive message for the day. Most decks come with a book explaining all the meanings, and there are tons of resources online, so you don't have to be an expert to use them. My favorite deck is *Beauty of the Tarot* by Brenda Villa.

Whatever you do, do not check your phone first thing in the morning. If the first thing you see when you wake up is a text message, a missed call from somebody, or even just a notification of how many unread emails you have in your inbox, then you'll feel like you're behind before you even begin your day. You'll also miss out on the valuable opportunity to receive intuitive messages from your dreams, because you'll forget them by the time you're done checking your phone. I know this can be challenging, especially if you use your phone as an alarm, but it's one of the most important practices I can recommend. I wrote about this in more detail in chapter 10.

The Practice

Pick one of the five recommended morning ritual ideas and commit to trying it before or after your Freedom Meditation practice. Pay attention to how it impacts your day, your mantra, and the quality of your meditation.

If you prefer to be guided through the audio version of this experience, go to justinmichaelwilliams.com/staywoke.

JOURNAL PROMPTS

1 Of the five recommended practices, which do you commit to trying this week?

2 When you feel like you don't have time for your morning practices, what is one thing you can remind yourself of that will inspire you to stay committed to your practice?

CIGARETTE BREAK MEDITATION

ANCHOR MANTRA

"I am connected. I am clear."

If smoking was meditation, cigarette smokers would be respected as the most dedicated, disciplined practitioners around. No matter where, no matter the circumstances, they will always find the time for a smoke. Try taking a cue from their devotion with a technique I call Cigarette Break Meditation. A Cigarette Break Meditation is a micromeditation that you can puff on for a few seconds or minutes whenever you need to reconnect to your spirit. Use it *in addition to* your daily practice—not to replace it.

You can practice Cigarette Break Meditations in your car, in the subway, in an elevator, or even in the middle of a heated argument to regain your composure. I use them to overcome writer's block, to make quick decisions, before I go on stage, before an important meeting, when I'm overwhelmed—the list is endless. Your skill will increase as your practice matures.

P.S. I don't condone smoking cigarettes, but Cigarette Break Meditations? I'll take a pack a day.

The Practice

Use this practice on the go anytime you need to center yourself. Close your eyes, place your hands over your heart, deepen your breath, and call forth the energy of your mantra. That's it. You can do this practice for anywhere between 30 seconds and 2 minutes. If you need a secondary mantra, use "I am connected. I am clear."

If you prefer to be guided through the audio version of this experience, go to justinmichaelwilliams.com/staywoke.

JOURNAL PROMPTS

1 Identify three recurring moments when you could benefit from using a Cigarette Break Meditation to center you during the day.

2 What is a signal that you need a Cigarette Break Meditation? Overwhelm? Exhaustion? Headache? Worry? Usually your body gives you a cue—what is it?

Your life purpose is not a job title.

I repeat: **Your life purpose is not a job title.**

Your purpose is not to be a singer, writer, artist, dancer, actor, yoga teacher, or entrepreneur. Those are all job titles. Those are all mediums through which you *express* purpose—and there will be many mediums through which you express purpose. So stop expecting to find a catchy one-liner with which to neatly package your purpose. Release yourself from the burden of thinking it will ever be that simple. All that searching, spinning, and obsessive thinking is keeping you from recognizing the purpose that's been expressing itself through you all along.

We all have many purposes throughout this Great Mystery of life. The key to finding yours is to stop searching, attune to what's in front of you, and ask: *How can I serve?*

Your purpose is not what you do, it's *why you do it*. This definition makes living with purpose a moment-to-moment practice. A practice of presence. A practice of awareness. And a practice of action.

Being of service is wired into the human experience, and it is the pathway to finding meaning and purpose in everything you do.[6]

YOUR LIFE PURPOSE IS *NOT* A JOB TITLE.

The Practice

Close your eyes, place your hands over your heart, and begin your Freedom Meditation practice using the anchor mantra "How can I serve?" Ask this question about your job, your relationship, or even the meeting you have coming up this week. If you ask, "How can I serve?" in every situation, you will find purpose in everything you do.

If you prefer to be guided through the audio version of this experience, go to justinmichaelwilliams.com/staywoke.

JOURNAL PROMPTS

I learned this exercise from my mentor and friend Chip Conley while attending a retreat at the Modern Elder Academy. What I love most is that you can use this exercise for different scenarios. Try it on your romantic relationship, your role as a parent, your job, or any aspect of life for which you're trying to find greater purpose and meaning.

1 Answer this question: What do you *really* do?

2 Then ask it again, from your heart: What do you *really* do? Go one layer deeper with a new answer.

   Then ask it again, going even deeper: What do you *really* do?

3 Keep asking yourself the question "What do you *really* do?," going deeper and deeper each time, until you have five to eight different answers. Remember, it's not about a job title or a catchy phrase. Try to find the essence.

4 Knowing what you know now, what is your purpose in relation to the situation you chose to focus on?

GET SH!T DONE

ANCHOR MANTRA

"I will not be distracted. This is my sacred time. I deserve this"
or "I call on you, Creative Spirit. I am here at your service."

This productivity hack from my mentor Lorin Roche changed my life so significantly that I share it with everybody I know. It's called Power Hours. Whether you're a full-time creative, working on a passion project, or have a day job, this tip will change the game.

Here's how to find your Power Hours:

1 Wake up and go to sleep around the same time every day for seven days. Try to stay as consistent as possible.

2 You may notice a two- to three-hour window each day when you experience a subtle lift in your mood and mind-set—when you feel most awake, alert, energized, and engaged.

3 Track the start and end time of that window every day for seven days. You can keep a log in your phone to make it easy.

4 You may notice two windows, one in the morning and one at night. If that's the case, track both.

5 At the end of the week, review your notes to see if you can find a pattern, a consistent window when you are the most alert and engaged. These are your Power Hours.

Your Power Hours are the period when your natural energy is the strongest, your mind is the most alert, and your brain is the most creative—so you should try to block this time out to do your most important work. .

I used my Power Hours to write this book, but if you're not working on a big creative project, just go back to the vision you wrote in chapter 2 and focus on a task that would bring you closer to your goals in any of the 5 Life Zones. If it's not realistic for you to work toward your personal goals during the day, then notice if you have a second set of Power Hours in the evening and use it. Most of us do. If you work a day job, then use your daytime Power Hours to complete the assignments you get evaluated on—the stuff that your boss cares about most—and your evening Power Hours to work toward your vision.

I realize that committing to three hours isn't realistic for everyone, so do your best to create even a small window each day to work on something that matters. Even fifteen minutes is better than nothing. During that time, tell everyone in your life you'll be unavailable so they don't freak out, turn your phone on airplane mode, and ditch all distractions. My entire life now revolves around my Power Hours so I can take full advantage of this creative window. This time is sacred, so try your best not to waste it.

The Practice

Always initiate your Power Hours with a meditation practice. You can use one of the following anchor mantras, depending on what you need that day.

Option 1 (for commitment): "I will not be distracted. This is my sacred time. I deserve this."

Option 2 (for creativity): "I call on you, Creative Spirit. I am here at your service."

If you prefer to be guided through the audio version of this experience, go to justinmichaelwilliams.com/staywoke

JOURNAL PROMPTS

1 When are your Power Hours?

2 What project could you work on during this window to get you closer to your vision and goals?

3 What parts of your current schedule make it difficult to take full advantage of your Power Hours? What adjustments can be made to accommodate your new commitment?

4 Whom do you need to notify about your new schedule so that you will feel supported?

5 How will making this daily commitment impact the trajectory of your life? What do you have to gain by doing it? What do you have to lose if you don't?

CHAPTER

15

ME TOO

ENVIRONMENTAL RIGHTS

social justice

LGBTQIA+

BLACK LIVES MATTER

I **will never forget the night Trump got elected as** the president of the United States of America, and I'm guessing you won't either. It knocked the wind out of me. I keeled over onto the floor of my sister's apartment in Los Angeles—facedown, heart in my stomach, feeling almost lifeless—as I heard the CNN narrator confirming the news over, and over, and over. I started having visions of our immigrant brothers and sisters hiding in back rooms, like in the story of Anne Frank, taking refuge in the annexes of our lives. I imagined the police coming to my door to check if I was hiding anyone and violently killing all who resisted the new world order. An entire horror film played out in my mind. I was scared. I was sad. But I wasn't in disbelief.

Something inside me always knew that hatred, racism, and bigotry were not as dead as they pretended to be. The fact that so many people voted for this man confirmed my fears. It shattered the illusion. It made me question everything. Were there really that many people who hated people like me? Who thought my lifestyle was wrong? Who valued money over lives? I spent the night crying, feeling helpless, and mourning the death of hope. But as the sun rose the next morning, something powerful happened: I, and thousands of other young people around the world, *woke up*. We stepped up to the front lines, ready to learn, and serve, and organize with the social justice warriors who had been fighting tirelessly for our rights for all these years.

Before Trump, I would've only considered myself a backseat activist— involved from a distance, attending the occasional rally or protest, priding myself in not watching the news because it was "too negative."

After Trump, the back seat was no longer an option. Experiencing the blatant disregard for black lives, the rise of white supremacists, the pain of the #MeToo movement, the hatred toward our immigrant brothers and sisters, children dying in the arms of our country, the destruction of our beautiful earth and oceans, and the gun violence taking innocent lives, I could no longer sit on the sidelines. I suddenly found myself in meetings, reading articles, having tough conversations,

WHEN WE
ALL COME TOGETHER,
WE ARE THE MAJORITY.

and trying to figure out what I could do to get involved in a meaningful way. It was overwhelming at first. I felt like such a novice. And I felt shame and guilt for not having gotten involved sooner. I didn't understand all the politics; I didn't know about all the organizations; I didn't know how I was going to find time in my schedule; and I didn't even know if what we were doing would make any impact at all—but I had to try.

As I said in the beginning of this book, being "woke" isn't just about knowledge. It is a call to action that arises from fearless awareness. Watching the news, reading articles, and talking with your friends is only step one of the process. The next step is action.

This quote from author Ethan Nichtern describes it perfectly: "Every time meditation is viewed as an act of 'tranquility,' there is a subtle political bias at play. Calmness is a great quality when it's appropriate to the situation at hand. But more deeply, meditation is about AWARENESS. Right now, awareness calls us to action."[1]

I know what it's like to feel helpless, overwhelmed, or lost when you're trying to get involved. I had so many questions. How do I stay engaged as an activist? How do I make space for all the difficult emotions being stirred up? How do I generate empathy for those I don't agree with? How do I check my own assumptions and false beliefs? And how do I practice self-care in the process?

The practices in this section are what helped me find my place in the social justice movement. My hope is that they help you find yours, too.

The system that keeps us separate is the system that keeps us broken. **When we *all* come together, we are the majority**. It's time for "the rest of us" to stand together as one and rise.

BECOME A BETTER ACTIVIST (A HOW-TO GUIDE)

ANCHOR MANTRA

"We deserve true equality."

On November 27, 2017, I sat on my patio to meditate, like I do most mornings. Being so close to the first anniversary of the Trump election, my centering question for the week was "How can I use my platform, my gifts, and my skills to contribute to the movement in an authentic way?"

And, like a lightning bolt, an idea hit me.

I heard a voice in my head say, "Twenty-eight days, twenty-eight interviews, with twenty-eight young black creators and leaders making history today." The voice was so clear that I knew I was being given a Divine assignment. Over the next twenty minutes, the idea continued to develop in my mind effortlessly—it was like someone had plugged a flash drive into my brain and initiated a large data transfer from the universe. I was being given every detail, every step, and every image; I even saw tag lines, commercials, and lists of potential guests. The assignment was clear: start a podcast and release one interview for every day of Black History Month.

And just like that, my podcast *Motivation for Black People* was born.

But I had never done a podcast before. I had no equipment. I wasn't well connected in the activist community. I didn't have any experience as an interviewer. And for God's sake, it was already November—how was I supposed to get twenty-eight interviews done by February 1? The excuses kicked in hard. But if I've learned one thing from all these years of meditating, it's that if you're lucky enough to hear the voice of God, you better listen. So I got started. I said, "YES." And this idea has taken me on one of the most fulfilling journeys of my life thus far. To date, we've inspired thousands of listeners from more than thirty different countries around the world to live better lives and brought relatable self-help to a community that is often shut out of the conversation. I've been blessed to interview some of the greatest thought leaders of our time, including Tarell Alvin McCraney, who won the Academy Award for his screenplay of *Moonlight*, which he adapted from his own play; Tarana Burke, founder of the Me Too movement; and Alicia Garza, cofounder of Black Lives Matter.

Alicia Garza told me something during our interview that I want to pass on to you. She had recently met a black dude who said, "I don't vote or get involved. I don't believe in these parties or these politicians, so the only thing I can do is improve myself." This prompted Alicia to pose a powerful question: "What is the consequence of not engaging at all?" She told me, "No change has ever happened, in the history of this country at least, by people just deciding to take care of themselves. If Harriet Tubman did that, we'd be in a very different place than we are today."[2]

Just taking care of yourself is not enough. We must stand together. We must lift one another up as a community. I understand there is corruption, I understand there is confusion, I understand there is anger. But, as Alicia asked so beautifully, what is the consequence of not engaging at all?

Getting involved in the social justice movement is not as challenging as you might think. Here are three steps you can follow, which we will investigate more deeply in our meditation practice:

STEP 1 Get clear on your values and vision for change.

STEP 2 Do a Google search to see if there are any organizations that align with your values and vision.

STEP 3 If there aren't any, start your own.

What is your vision for equality? How can you contribute to change? Let's explore.

The Practice

Place your hands over your lower belly, below your navel. Take several deep breaths and initiate the anchor mantra "We deserve true equality." You may feel an intense wave of emotion—try to sit with it. Remember, healthy anger is not bad. The energy of anger can be channeled into growth and change. Welcome whatever arises.

If you prefer to be guided through the audio version of this experience, go to justinmichaelwilliams.com/staywoke.

JOURNAL PROMPTS

1 Who is the "we" you are referring to in your mantra?

2 What are you passionate about? What pisses you off about the world? What lights you up? Makes you angry? What makes you weep? These are your justice values.

3 What is your vision for change? What does a brighter future look like to you?

4 What organizations align with your vision and justice values? If you can't think of any, do a Google search.

5 If you don't find an organization that aligns with your mission, what would it take to start something of your own? Who could help you? Remember, you can start small in your local community.

THE FIRST STEP TO RADICAL CHANGE

ANCHOR MANTRA

"I am ready to change. Show me the way."

The first step most of us take when trying to grow or change is to look for support from the outside. We look for the next self-help book, the next inspiring podcast, the next fad diet, or the next online course that claims to magically change your life in twenty-one days. But none of those external changes will ever have a lasting impact if you don't understand this: real change is not just about what you do but about *who you are*.

If we try to initiate change from the outside in, we may be inspired for a few days or weeks, at best, but we always end up returning to our default mode after the high wears off. When we initiate transformation from the inside out, we change the core of who we are, which in turn affects our actions, choices, and the trajectory of our lives.

Take a moment to think about how you show up in the world. Who are you *for real*? What kind of friend are you? What kind of coworker are you? What kind of lover are you? How are you to your own self? And I'm not talking about who you portray yourself to be on social media. I'm talking about the person you are in private, when no one else is looking.

This is inner activism. It's about you, your vibration, and taking responsibility for the energy you bring to the world. Let's dive in.

The Practice

Place your hands over your chest, close your eyes, take a few breaths, and drop into your heart. Use this anchor mantra: "I am ready to change. Show me the way." And listen closely. Try to feel it instead of overthinking it. This practice is about being compassionate, yet radically transparent, raw, and honest with yourself. That's where lasting change begins.

If you prefer to be guided through the audio version of this experience, go to justinmichaelwilliams.com/staywoke.

JOURNAL PROMPTS

1 What changes do you most want to see in the world?
2 What do you need to change about your own self, internally, to match that vision for change?
3 How will making that transformation shift your everyday life?

REAL CHANGE IS NOT JUST ABOUT WHAT YOU DO BUT ABOUT *WHO YOU ARE.*

UNCOVER YOUR HIDDEN PREJUDICES

"I'm sorry. I can do better. May you be happy.
May you be free. May we both find peace."

"If we can only name the feet that are situated on our necks,
but fail to name and recognize the ways our feet our
situated on someone else's neck, we will never, ever be free."

DARNELL L. MOORE[3]

If you're fighting for #BlackLivesMatter but afraid of a trans person in your restroom . . .

If you support the #MeToo movement but think it's "too confusing" to have so many gender pronouns . . .

If you're working to save the environment but annoyed when people make such a "big deal" about cultural appropriation . . .

If you hold up a rainbow flag at the pride parade but have racist dating preferences . . .

If you went to college to get an education but forget where you came from . . .

If you're a person who says, "I don't see color," "I don't see race," "We are all one" . . .

. . . you have some work to do.

I'm not saying this in a blaming or shaming way—we all do.

Social justice work isn't just about the outer work. It's not just about holding up flags, raising your fist, shouting in protest, or attending a march. That's the easy part. The revolution happens in the secret spaces of your life, when no one else is around. How are you treating others? What are you doing to help the homeless in your neighborhood? What comments are you saying in private when you don't understand someone else's point of view?

The person who helped me grow the most as it relates to this topic is my brother and fellow author Darnell L. Moore. He was the first person I ever interviewed for my podcast, *Motivation for Black People*. In that episode, he gave three tips that I want to share with you. They're relevant to all of us.

1 **Commit to a practice of self-reflection**, specifically about social justice. Oftentimes, we do to others what the system has done to us. I know that's a hard pill to swallow, but that's why meditation is so important. It can unveil the ways in which you are a part of the problem. This will require you to sit in discomfort, but it's necessary. Full accountability is the first step toward meaningful change.

2 **Study.** Google is a wonderful thing. Use it. Learn the history of the movement you're a part of. See what worked and what didn't, so you can avoid repeating the same cycles. We often think we're trying something new, but our ancestors have been down this road before. Learn from them.

3 **Don't be a brand—make an impact.** Just because you get thousands of likes on your social media posts doesn't mean you're making the world a better place. How are you contributing to your family? To your local community? What are you doing in private when no one else is watching? It's easy to get lost in the illusion of who you've presented yourself to be online and pretend you're making a greater impact than you actually are. The work you do on the ground, as an individual, is more important than what you post online. Get off your phone, get outside, and do the work.[4]

The following practice and journal prompts will jump-start the awareness process. After that, it's up to you to take action.

The Practice

Close your eyes, place your hands over your lower belly, and think of a community that you have joked about, marginalized, discriminated against, or left behind. Begin your Freedom Meditation practice using the suggested anchor mantra, "I'm sorry. I can do better. May you be happy. May you be free. May we both find peace." See what arises.

If you prefer to be guided through the audio version of this experience, go to justinmichaelwilliams.com/staywoke.

JOURNAL PROMPTS

1 In what specific ways is your life out of alignment with the freedom you desire for the world? What do you need to change?

2 Whose neck are your feet on? Whom are you marginalizing, even slightly, without realizing it?

3 What's a step you can commit to taking within the next thirty days to learn more about the community you wrote about in the previous question?

WE'RE ALL PRIVILEGED:
THIS TEST WILL TELL YOU HOW MUCH

ANCHOR MANTRA

"How can I help? Show me the way."

"Privilege isn't about what you've gone through;
it's about what you haven't had to go through."
JANAYA "FUTURE" KHAN
COFOUNDER, BLACK LIVES MATTER TORONTO[5]

My biggest lesson on privilege came through a YouTube video. It showed a mixed-race group of young people doing an exercise called the Privilege Walk (you can do a quick YouTube search to find it). In the video, the facilitator asked participants questions about their lives. Participants were then told to take a step forward or a step backward, depending on their answers. Each step forward got you closer to "success," while each step backward took you further away. Everyone started on the same line, but by the end of the video, the differences in privilege were painfully obvious.[6]

Let's try it together. I have created a new version of the Privilege Walk for this book. I am going to mark all of the statements below with my personal responses: +1 for a step forward, -1 for a step back, and 0 for no movement. You do the same. At the end of the exercise, add up your numbers.

If your parents worked nights and weekends to support your family,
   take one step back.
   JMW = -1, You = _____

If you are able to move through the world without fear of sexual assault,
   take one step forward.
   JMW = 0, You = _____

If you are cisgender (meaning your gender identity corresponds to your birth sex),
   take one step forward.
   JMW = +1, You − _____

If you can show affection for your romantic partner in public without fear of
   ridicule or violence, take one step forward.
   JMW = 0, You = _____

If you have ever been diagnosed as having a physical or mental illness/disability, take one step back.

JMW = 0, You = _____

If the primary language spoken in your household growing up was not English, take one step back.

JMW = 0, You = _____

If you have ever tried to change your speech or mannerisms to gain credibility, take one step back.

JMW = -1, You = _____

If you can go anywhere in the country and easily find the kinds of hair products you need and/or cosmetics that match your skin color, take one step forward.

JMW = 0, You = _____

If you can pass as heterosexual, take one step forward.

JMW = 0, You = _____

If you were embarrassed about your clothes or house while growing up, take one step back.

JMW = -1, You = _____

If you can make mistakes and not have people attribute your behavior to flaws in your racial/gender group, take one step forward.

JMW = 0, You = _____

If you can legally marry the person you love, regardless of where you live, take one step forward.

JMW = 0, You = _____

If you were born in the United States, take one step forward.

JMW = +1, You = _____

If you or your parents have ever gone through a divorce, take one step back.

JMW = -1, You = _____

If you felt like you had adequate access to healthy food growing up, take one step forward.

JMW = 0, You = _____

If you are reasonably sure you would be hired for a job on the basis of your abilities and qualifications, take one step forward.
JMW = 0, You = _____

If you would never think twice about calling the police when trouble occurs, take one step forward.
JMW = 0, You = _____

If you can see a doctor whenever you feel the need, take one step forward.
JMW = +1, You = _____

If you feel comfortable being emotionally expressive/open, take one step forward.
JMW = 0, You = _____

If you have ever been the only person of your race/gender/socioeconomic status/sexual orientation in a classroom or workplace setting, please take one step back.
JMW = -1, You = _____

If you have a college education, take one step forward.
JMW = +1, You = _____

If you took out loans for your education, take one step back.
JMW = -1, You = _____

If you get time off for your religious holidays, take one step forward.
JMW = +1, You = _____

If you feel comfortable walking home alone at night, take one step forward.
JMW = 0, You = _____

If you have ever traveled outside the United States, take one step forward.
JMW = +1, You = _____

If you feel confident that your parents would be able to financially help/support you if you were going through a monetary hardship, take one step forward.
JMW = 0, You = _____

If you have ever been bullied or made fun of because of something that you can't change, take one step back.
JMW = -1, You = _____

If there were more than fifty books in your house growing up, take one step forward.

    JMW = 0, You = _____

If you studied the culture or the history of your ancestors in elementary school, take one step forward.

    JMW = +1, You = _____

If your parents or guardians attended college, take one step forward.

    JMW = 0, You = _____

If you ever went on a family vacation, take one step forward.

    JMW = +1, You = _____

If one of your parents was ever laid off or unemployed not by choice, take one step back.

    JMW = -1, You = _____

If you were ever uncomfortable about a joke or a statement you overheard related to your race, ethnicity, gender, appearance, or sexual orientation but felt unsafe to confront the situation, take one step back.

    JMW = -1, You = _____

If you have access to clean water, take one step forward.

    JMW = +1, You = _____

My score = 0, Your score = _____
(Lowest possible = -11, Highest possible = +23)

The goal of this exercise is not to compare us, but to illustrate that privilege and oppression are nonbinary. Yes, I am a mostly gay black man who grew up in a broken home—but I also had several +1s on my list. We all have privilege; some of us just have more than others.

The following practice and journal prompts will help you *feel* the ways in which you are privileged and explore how you can use those privileges to heal the world.

The Practice

Review your responses to the Privilege Walk exercise, then place your palms down on your knees and close your eyes. Drop this anchor mantra into your Freedom Meditation practice without judgment: "How can I help? Show me the way."

Welcome what arises. Then move into action and help.

If you prefer to be guided through the audio version of this experience, go to justinmichaelwilliams.com/staywoke.

JOURNAL PROMPTS

The following questions apply to everyone, regardless of how high or low you scored on the Privilege Walk. The goal is to cross-pollinate and gain greater understanding of those who are different than you so that you can learn how to serve and help.

1 What's an easy way you can use your advantages to help those in need?

2 If you are usually in the majority everywhere you go, where can you go within the next thirty days where you are not the majority? Is there a community organization, church, rally, or social meetup you can attend where you feel like an outsider?

3 What fears arise when you think about attending the event in question 2?

4 How can you flip those fears into questions of curiosity? What could you *learn* in spite of your fear? What's the best possible outcome?

A SELF-CARE PRACTICE FOR ACTIVISTS

ANCHOR MANTRA

"I am full power. I am light."

We are warriors for peace. Warriors for love. Warriors for change. Warriors for equality. But we must also tend to the wars within.

When you do not care for yourself, you internalize the same oppression that you are fighting against. When you are exhausted, your capacity for compassion is limited. When you are out of alignment, it's hard to make the right choices, especially when you're under pressure.

I know you're spending time organizing, and learning, and marching, and defending, and protesting, and bringing people together. I know it might feel like taking time for your self-care is stealing valuable time away from doing the actual *work*, but we need our warriors bright—and not just for your own sake.

We need you so grounded that we feel safe following your lead.

We need you so centered that you never stray from your values and vision.

We need you so rested that you do not lash out at others during times of stress.

We need you to shine your light so brightly that anyone who is lost can find you.

You are a lighthouse. Your healing is essential to the liberation of the people.

The Practice

Start your practice with the 6 Count Breath. Inhale for 6 counts, hold for 6, and exhale for 6. This practice will rapidly regulate your nervous system, so it's especially useful during times of high stress. Repeat the 6 Count Breath at least five times before you start your meditation. It's going to feel long at first, but try to stick with it.

After the 6 Count Breath, bring your body to a place of rest and begin your Freedom Meditation practice. Use the suggested anchor mantra: "I am full power. I am light."

If you prefer to be guided through the audio version of this experience, go to justinmichaelwilliams.com/staywoke.

JOURNAL PROMPTS

1 How did you feel after the 6 Count Breath?

2 What is one easy way you can practice better self-care? Sometimes it's as simple as remembering to eat, turning your phone to silent, or going to sleep earlier.

3 How does taking time for your self-care empower you to be a more effective healer and leader?

**YOU ARE A LIGHTHOUSE.
YOUR HEALING IS ESSENTIAL TO THE
LIBERATION OF THE PEOPLE.**

MEDITATING WHILE BLACK . . . OR GAY, OR TRANS, OR [INSERT MARGINALIZED VOICE HERE]

ANCHOR MANTRA

"We are the revolution."

When I was preparing to record my album, I felt like there was something in my subconscious holding me back, and I couldn't quite put my finger on what it was. Several of my friends recommended hypnosis. Since I'm a guy who likes to try everything, I decided to give it a shot. This was my first time getting hypnotized, so I was a little scared. I didn't know what to expect. Was she going to pull out one of those black and white spinning balls on a string? Would I remember anything? Would it even work on me?

Next thing you know, I was in a trance. When I woke up, I was holding a piece of paper and a red crayon; apparently the hypnotherapist had asked me to draw something. I looked down at what I drew and was shocked.

It was a burning red swastika—the symbol of white supremecy. A symbol that represented, among many other things, the powers that held my ancestors back from their dreams, goals, and aspirations for centuries.

In that instant, I understood that intergenerational trauma is real.

Science has proven that we inherit trauma from our ancestors. It's encoded in our DNA. This is why meditating while black (or gay, or poor, or trans, or [insert marginalized voice here]) is revolutionary. If you meditate when you're marginalized, you'll start to break free from the chains that keep you in your place. The fact that we even have the opportunity to worry about our mental health, what we are manifesting, and our life purpose is a privilege that we cannot take for granted. My soul sister and founder of Curvy, Curly, Conscious, Shelah Marie, once said to me, "We are the first generation of healers." I'd like to take that a step further and say we are the first generation with a chance to *break the cycles*. Meditation is just step one. It gives you awareness so you can take the biggest, most important step: action.

It's time to drop the story of your not-enoughness and awaken to your brilliance. If enough of us do that, there will be a revolution.

This is our time to wake up, my brothers and sisters. This is our time to rise. And we rise together.

The Practice

Hold your hands open in front of you, palms facing upward, like you are holding a large tray. Your arms can be bent and relaxed, with your elbows resting by your sides. Close your eyes and visualize your ancestors (either figurative or literal)—the people who came before you. Initiate the anchor mantra "We are the revolution." Begin your Freedom Meditation practice.

If you prefer to be guided through the audio version of this experience, go to justinmichaelwilliams.com/staywoke.

JOURNAL PROMPTS

1 What oppressive cycles might you be repeating from your family or ancestors?

2 Of these patterns, which is holding you back most?

3 What support do you need to break this pattern? What do you need to learn? Once you answer this question, you can research healers, books, blogs, and podcasts to help you grow.

IT'S TIME TO DROP THE STORY OF YOUR NOT-ENOUGHNESS AND AWAKEN TO YOUR BRILLIANCE.

TOGETHER: MOVING BEYOND IDENTITY

ANCHOR MANTRA

"I am you. You are me. We are we. I commit to thee."

Even though most of us despise racism and prejudice, research has proven that we're all a little bit racist sometimes. We all make negative and positive assumptions about other people based on superficial differences in appearance and social identity. It happens when an Asian driver cuts you off on the highway, when a homeless person asks you for money, or when you see a group of black guys standing on the corner and you get extra cautious. This is called *implicit bias*, and it's happening in us subconsciously all the time. However, numerous studies show that even a brief mindfulness meditation practice can interrupt that pattern. One study in particular proved that after a ten-minute mindfulness meditation practice, people demonstrated less implicit bias toward blacks and elderly people.[7] This gives us hope. We can undo this pattern—and meditation can help.

I'll close this chapter with another quote from Janaya "Future" Khan: "I want us to get to a place where our identity is not informing our politics. . . . Our identities, that might be a good entry point, but we can't stay there. . . . All I'm doing if I'm only fighting for Black people is reframing colonialism so it's more convenient for someone like me."[8]

This doesn't mean you don't fight for your people, but don't let your people be the only ones you're fighting for.

Do you stand with the homeless? Do you stand with the LGBTQIA+ community? Do you stand with the trans community? Do you stand with the Native people of our land? Do you stand with the water protectors? Do you stand with the white, Jewish, Asian, Latinx, Indian, black, and brown people and all those in between?

I feel like one of the biggest problems in the world is that when we see something going on that doesn't apply to us (or, rather, that we *think* doesn't apply to us), we ignore it. We ignore shootings that are not in our country. We ignore disasters that are not happening to our community. And we ignore inequality that doesn't affect our personal freedom. We need to change that.

We must come together.

The liberation of every one of our groups is integral to the liberation of us all—all identities, all races, all religions, all genders, all creeds, and all socioeconomic backgrounds. In order to find *true* equality, we must stand together. We need to take time to understand people who are not like us.

Let this practice be that opportunity for you.

The Practice

Place your hands over your heart, close your eyes, and drop this anchor mantra into your Freedom Meditation practice: "I am you. You are me. We are we. I commit to thee." I like to whisper the words to myself, imagining I'm speaking to all people, plants, and animals of the world.

> If you prefer to be guided through the audio version of this experience, go to justinmichaelwilliams.com/staywoke.

JOURNAL PROMPTS

1 Is there a community whose struggle you do not understand?

2 Imagine you're sitting face-to-face with a member of the community you identified in the previous question. What questions would you ask them to learn more about their struggle?

3 What values or goals might you have in common with that community? How are you similar?

4 Take your responses from question 2 and do some research on Google to see if you can find answers *written by people in the community* (not outside opinions). This will help you deepen your compassion and understanding.

I AM YOU.
YOU ARE ME.
WE ARE WE.
I COMMIT TO THEE.

closing anthem

tried for weeks to come up with something ultrainspirational to say to you at the end of this book. I wrote pages and pages, and nothing felt quite right. And then I figured out why . . .

I am supposed to sing you a song.

I wrote this song on a night when I was feeling alone, when I was comparing myself to other people, when I wished I was further along in my process, when I was watching other people going to parties and events, getting awards, and taking fabulous trips with their gorgeous partners, while I sat in my room alone, wondering, "Why am I not there yet?"

I closed my eyes to meditate, and a vision appeared. It was little Justin. A boy who wanted so badly to be seen and heard. A boy who wanted to be accepted and loved for who he really was and not just for his achievements. A boy who never stopped whispering to me, who never stopped begging me to go after my "impossible" dream. It seems no matter how much I meditate or how much I achieve, that little boy is always inside me, wanting to be loved. So I wrote this song for him—and for the child inside each of us who just wants to hear, "You are enough." I invite you to sing along with me. You can find the song on any music platform by searching for "I Am Enough" by Justin Michael Williams.

I AM ENOUGH

Little boy, don't cry
You been in pain
Enough

Little girl, don't fight
You're finally safe
Enough

One day I'll look into your eyes
Show you you don't need hide behind disguise

Spread your wings, you're terrified
Don't be afraid, you're born to fly
I'm by your side

I am enough
I am golden, baby, yeah
I am enough
I am enough

Little girl it's alright
You've taken the blame
Enough

Little boy don't hide
You been ashamed
Enough

One day I'll look into your eyes
Show you you don't need hide behind disguise

Spread your wings, you're terrified
Don't be afraid, you're born to fly
I'm by your side

I am enough
I am golden, baby, yeah
I am enough
I am enough

If I can feel this,
All this emotion
Will it be poison?
Or will I grow?

Can you heal this?
Or am I broken?
Hear me screaming
Make me whole

I am enough
I am golden, baby, yeah
I am enough
I am enough

You are enough
You are golden, baby, yeah
You are enough
You are enough

We are enough
We are golden, baby, yes
We are enough
We are enough

We are enough.

. . .

May you go after your dreams.

May you never give up.

May meditation be a safe space for you to heal. For you
to grow. And for you to wake up to the dream—to the *real
dream*—that's always been inside of you.

I thank you. I honor you. I bow to you.

I love you.

xo

Justin Michael Williams

the gratitude list

Since this is my first book, I'm taking the liberty of writing
acknowledgments like they're a long-winded Grammy Awards acceptance
speech. You can go ahead and cue the music, but I ain't stoppin'!

I would like to thank . . .

BACA: I know you never like to take credit, but I wouldn't be the man I am
today if it weren't for you. Thank you for letting me talk about you over and over
and over with audiences around the world. You are and will always be one of
the greatest gifts of my life. Thank you for always bringing me back to God. For
reminding me what's important. For teaching me how to listen. For passing on your
wisdom. I'm so lucky to be your grandson. I love you so much.

LORIN ROCHE, my friend, my teacher, my guide, and my first mentor
after my Baca passed away: You took the torch and fanned it with your endless
generosity. Without you and your knowledge and your willingness to take me
under your wing, none of this would exist. Thank you for giving me the freedom to
pass along your teachings. What you taught me was more than just meditation—
you brought me home to myself. And for that, I thank you.

ZHENA MUZYKA: I'm raising my teacup and toasting to your magic and
brilliance. Thank you for taking a risk and saying, "Yes!" to the young black boy
with big dreams. For the title. For standing by my side even when this book left
your hands. You are a *visionnaire.* You were the first person to believe in me as an
author. You helped me see myself and how important this book was for the world.

GARETH ESERSKY, my literary agent: Working with you and the Carol Mann Agency has been, hands down, one of the best working relationships of my life. I cannot possibly thank you enough. Resting in the embrace of your zest and expertise made this process one of the most fun and memorable moments of my career thus far.

JENNIFER Y. BROWN: There is no one else in the entire universe who could've edited this book but you. I will never forget the goose bumps I felt after our first call—a perfect match, total alignment. Thank you and the entire team at Sounds True for bringing the vision of *Stay Woke* to life. Sounds True authors wrote many of the books that have changed my life most, and it is a great honor to say that I am now one of them.

VICTORIA CASSINOVA: There are no words to justly describe the magnitude of your artistry and talent but, even more importantly, of your heart. The art you created for this book has shifted culture. For the first time ever, our people can see themselves represented as a part of this movement. You are making history, and we are all so lucky to experience your magic.

DACHER KELTNER, my brother: I am blown away by you. You've shown up with such selfless and sincere devotion not only to me and this book but to all people who are overcoming the struggle. Thank you for believing in my voice. For showing me how to merge science and heart. And for taking the time out of your busy schedule to read my manuscript and provide such detailed notes. You are an angel, and the support you have shown me throughout this process is unparalleled.

ALEX CAPRIOTTI, KERRI FRANCES, DARNELL L. MOORE, DARNELL WALKER, ERIC WILLIAMS—my first readers: Thank you for saying yes to such a *big ask*. Your love is embedded into the heart of this book.

ERIN FALCONER: Thank you for reappearing in my life at such a pivotal moment. Thank you for your sage advice and for contributing your mommy magic to this book. You are one of the most incredible women I know.

CHIP CONLEY, my soul brother: Thank you for helping me to get this book into the hands of all the right people— people whom I would've never met. Thank you for asking me that important question, "How can I support you in doing the best work of your life?" It is a great honor to call you a mentor and friend.

To all the people who helped me market and promote this book: I couldn't have dreamed of a more masterful team to help me bring *Stay Woke* to the world. I feel so blessed. Thank you from the bottom of my heart.

To every student who has been in class with me: Thank you for allowing me to listen to your hearts. Without your tough questions and the wisdom of your vulnerability, there would be no *Stay Woke*.

To my mom, **BARBARA**: You are the definition of the word "service." What you've done and sacrificed for me and our family goes beyond the call of duty. You have endured so much, yet you still keep such a bright spirit and your eyes toward joy and possibility. Thank you for always believing in me and for allowing me to be so open about our story—I know the world is a better place because of it. Thank you for growing with me. Thank you for learning with me. Thank you for trusting me through every risk I've taken since college. I love you.

To my dad, **TERRANCE**: When people ask who I get all my talent from, I point to you! I'm so grateful for this incredible relationship we're building as men, which has gone deeper than I ever thought possible. We are strong. We are triumphant. We are Williamses. I love you.

To my **PAPA TYRONE**, my **NANA**, my siblings **TERRANCE JR.**, **JESSICA**, **ANTHONY**, and **DESTINEE**, and my entire family, which is way too large to list: What a journey it has been! And I couldn't have asked for a better family to take this wild ride with. I have grown so much through the love and connection we share. Each of you has shaped and molded me in more ways than you could ever know. I love you.

ERROL BUNTUYAN, CRISTI CHRISTENSEN, RUSH DAVIS, JEREMY ERWIN, RYAN GOOD, DARAIHA GREENE, MARY HABERSKI, VANESSA INN, MIKE and **JENNIFER LANE, JANE LEE, JELANI LEGOHN, SIANNA SHERMAN, TIM TATTERSALL, KIT TODD, KOYA WEBB, HELEN VASQUEZ, AND RAYE ZARAGOZA**: *Thank you for teaching me how to love Justin.* Thank you for giving me permission to be flaky, to go on "do not disturb" for nine whole months, and for being by my side through every experiment and realization on this messy, magical, and sometimes isolating journey. Your support, your space, your presence, your texts, and your love have made it safe for me to transform into the real me. *I love you all so fucking much.*

BRENDA VILLA: You are an angel. Thank you for your heart, your magic, your endless wisdom, and the way you lovingly call me out on *all my bullshit*. That seminal moment at your kitchen table was an initiation for me—a rite of passage. You showed me the doorway to my truth and inspired me to take responsibility and walk through it. I love you. I am so lucky to have you as a friend.

OPRAH: Thank you for showing me what's possible. You have created doorways in places where there were only walls. Thank you for carving a path for people like me. And most of all, thank you for being my mentor without even knowing it.

ESALEN. My favorite place in the world. I wrote my proposal on your lawn, dreamed up *Stay Woke* in your waters, and signed my first book deal at the edge of your cliffs. Thank you for your majestic beauty. You are my refuge, my safe place, and my sacred space.

And lastly to **GOD**, **SPIRIT**, **THE PRESENCE**, **THE UNIVERSE**, **THE ANGELS**, **GUIDES**, **ANCESTORS**, and **GUARDIANS** of this project: We did it! Thank you for protecting me, for protecting this project, for showing me the power of discipline and commitment, and for incubating my life so that I could be at your service, in full devotion. You have called me deeper inward and further forward than I've ever gone before. Thank you for teaching me to surrender and to trust. Thank you for showing up every day at 11:00 a.m. for our scheduled writing appointments. Thank you for proving to me again and again that the most important relationship in life is the one I have with myself and with Spirit. I am yours.

TO ALL OF YOU . . .

I thank you. I honor you. I love you.

daily practice plan

T his 40-day plan provides a powerful and structured way to experience Practices for Your Life. You can use it to coincide with your Freedom Meditation ~~Challenge~~ *Experiment* or anytime you need a motivational jump-start. The practices have been thoughtfully ordered to guide you through a transformational journey of radical internal, external, and social change. Every fifth day, you will return to the Daily Meditation Ritual and unique mantra you created in part 1. This will help you integrate all the new lessons into your personal practice.

If you don't resonate with one of the suggested minipractices, skip it and do your Daily Meditation Ritual instead. Remember, my recipes *always* welcome your substitutions.

297

goodies

EXTRAS TO HELP YOU ON YOUR PATH TO AWAKENING

To access all the free resources from this book, visit: justinmichaelwilliams.com/staywoke

Ritual tools—the best resource for Meditation Ritual Kits, crystals, and sustainable energy tools: justinmichaelwilliams.com/ritualkits

To work more closely with me at events, retreats, or speaking engagements, visit: justinmichaelwilliams.com

There's nothing I love more than getting to meet my readers.
Come say hello to me on social media: @wejustwill.

Listen to my podcast: motivationforblackpeople.com.

I have also created several online courses for you, including:

Meditation for the People

Spirit Academy: Mystical Teachings for Everyday People

How to Find Your Purpose and Make Money Doing What You Love (with Malcolm "MJ" Harris)

10 Steps to Self-Love (with Shelah Marie)

Astrology Made Easy: Discover Your Life's Purpose (with Mecca Woods)

They are all available at Courses4theCulture.com.

Join the movement to bring meditation to youth and young adults in need: StayWokeGiveBack.com.

Many incredible healers, teachers, and guides have helped me along my path to awakening. I want to make sure you have access to them too. Here are some of my faves.

Become certified to teach meditation: Lorin Roche and Camille Maurine, Radiance Sutras Meditation Teacher Training, MeditationTT.com

My all-time favorite yoga teacher: Sianna Sherman, Rasa Yoga, SiannaSherman.com

Magic, tarot, and intuitive wisdom: Brenda Villa, BrendaVilla.com

Trauma, healing, and shadow work: Robert Augustus Masters, RobertMasters.com (his book *Bringing Your Shadow Out of the Dark* is life-changing)

The science of living a meaningful life: Dacher Keltner and the Greater Good Science Center at University of California, Berkeley, ggsc.berkeley.edu

For those claiming their power as mentors and wisdom keepers: Chip Conley and the Modern Elder Academy, ChipConley.com

My favorite books:

Rising Strong by Brené Brown

Big Magic by Elizabeth Gilbert

The War of Art by Steven Pressfield

The Radiance Sutras by Lorin Roche

A New Earth by Eckhart Tolle (my first-ever spiritual book!)

The Wisdom of Sundays by Oprah Winfrey

notes

WE ARE THE REVOLUTION

1. "Mindfulness: Why Practice It?," *Greater Good Magazine*, greatergood.berkeley.edu/topic/mindfulness/definition#why-practice-mindfulness.

CHAPTER 2: WE HAVE A DREAM

1. Eva Clay, phone interview, November 17, 2018.

2. Martin Luther King Jr., *A Testament of Hope*, ed. James Melvin Washington (New York: HarperCollins, 1991).

3. Amy Wrzesniewski et al., "Jobs, Careers, and Callings: People's Relations to Their Work," *Journal of Research in Personality* 31 (1997): 21–33, faculty.som.yale.edu/amywrzesniewski/documents/Jobscareersandcallings.pdf.

4. Brent D. Rosso, Kathryn H. Dekas, and Amy Wrzesniewski, "On the Meaning of Work: A Theoretical Integration and Review," *Research in Organizational Behavior* 30 (2010): 91–127, doi.org/10.1016/j.riob.2010.09.001.

CHAPTER 3: WE STOP SELF-SABOTAGE

1. Yung Pueblo (@YungPueblo), Twitter, October 9, 2017, 9:22 a.m., twitter.com/YungPueblo/status/917424920916787201?s=20.

2. Ethan Kross et al., "Facebook Use Predicts Declines in Subjective Well-Being in Young Adults," *PLoS ONE* 8 (August 14, 2013): e69841, doi.org/10.1371/journal.pone.0069841.

3. Matthew Walker, *Why We Sleep* (New York: Scribner, 2017).

4. Kristin Neff, "Self-Compassion: An Alternative Conceptualization of a Healthy Attitude Toward Oneself," *Self and Identity* 2 (2003): 85–101, self-compassion.org/wp-content/uploads/publications/SCtheoryarticle.pdf.

5. Holly Yan, "'Hero' Security Guard Killed by Police Was Working Extra Shifts for His Son's Christmas," CNN, November 15, 2018, cnn.com/2018/11/15/us/chicago-area-security-guard-police-shooting/index.html.

6. Daniel Golden, *The Price of Admission* (New York: Crown, 2006).

7. Daniel Kahneman and Angus Deaton, "High Income Improves Evaluation of Life but Not Emotional Well-Being," *PNAS Early Edition*, August 4, 2010, doi.org/10.1073/pnas.1011492107.

8. Robert Augustus Masters, *To Be a Man* (Boulder, CO: Sounds True, 2015).

9. Arielle Ford, personal conversation, April 7, 2019.

CHAPTER 4: WE CHILL THE F*CK OUT

1. Jennifer E. Stellar et al., "Affective and Physiological Responses to the Suffering of Others: Compassion and Vagal Activity," *Journal of Personality and Social Psychology* 108, no. 4 (2015): 572–85, dx.doi.org/10.1037/pspi0000010.

CHAPTER 5: WE FREE OUR MINDS

1. James J. Gross, "Emotion Regulation: Affective, Cognitive, and Social Consequences," *Psychophysiology* 39 (2002): 281–91, doi.org/10.1017/s0048577201393198.

CHAPTER 7: WE PRACTICE PRESENCE

1. James L. Gross, "Emotion Regulation."

2. Ed Halliwell, "Can Meditation Help You with Depression?" *Greater Good Magazine*, October 5, 2018, greatergood.berkeley.edu/article/item/can_meditation_help_you_with_depression.

3. Jordi Quoidbach et al., "Emodiversity and the Emotional Ecosystem," *Journal of Experimental Psychology* 143, no. 6 (2014): 2057–66, dx.doi.org/10.1037/a0038025.

4. Kira M. Newman, "Five Science-Backed Strategies to Build Resilience," *Greater Good Magazine*, November 9, 2016, greatergood.berkeley.edu/article/item/five_science_backed_strategies_to_build_resilience.

CHAPTER 9: WE WANT ANSWERS

1. Hooria Jazaieri, "Can Mindfulness Improve Decision Making?," *Greater Good Magazine*, May 12, 2014, greatergood.berkeley.edu/article/item/can_mindfulness_improve_decision_making.

CHAPTER 10: WE BUILD RITUALS

1. Alison Wood Brooks et al., "Don't Stop Believing: Rituals Improve Performance by Decreasing Anxiety," *Organizational Behavior and Human Decision Processes* 137 (2016): 71–85, dx.doi.org/10.1016/j.obhdp.2016.07.004.

2. Shawn Achor and Michelle Gielan, "Consuming Negative News Can Make You Less Effective at Work," *Harvard Business Review*, September 14, 2015, hbr.org/2015/09/consuming-negative-news-can-make-you-less-effective-at-work.

3. Lars-Olov Lundqvist et al., "Emotional Responses to Music: Experience, Expression, and Physiology," *Psychology of Music* 37, no. 1 (2009): 61–90, doi.org/10.1177/0305735607086048.

CHAPTER 11: WE COMMIT

1. Maxwell Maltz, *Psycho-Cybernetics* (New York: Perigree, 2015).

2. Phillippa Lally et al., "How Are Habits Formed: Modelling Habit Formation in the Real World," *European Journal of Social Psychology* 40 (2010): 998–1009, doi.org/abs/10.1002/ejsp.674.

CHAPTER 12: MEDITATIONS FOR ANXIETY AND STRESS

1. Daniel Kahneman and Angus Deaton, "High Income Improves Evaluation of Life but Not Emotional Well-Being," *PNAS Early Edition*, August 4, 2010, doi.org/10.1073/pnas.1011492107.

2. Elizabeth Dunn and Michael Norton, *Happy Money* (New York: Simon and Schuster, 2013).

3. Matthew Walker, *Why We Sleep*.

4. "Lee Hecht Harrison Poll Finds Most Workers Losing Sleep Due to Work Related Stress," Lee Hecht Harrison (website), press release, April 27, 2015, lhh.com/us/en/about-us /press-room/2015/lee-hecht-harrison-poll-finds-most-workers-losing-sleep-due-to-work -related-stress.

5. Stacey Kennelly, "10 Steps to Savoring the Good Things in Life," *Greater Good Magazine*, July 23, 2012, greatergood.berkeley.edu/article /item/10_steps_to_savoring_the_good_things_in_life.

6. Summer Allen, *The Science of Gratitude* (white paper, Greater Good Science Center, Berkeley, California, May 2018), ggsc.berkeley.edu/images/uploads/GGSC-JTF_White_Paper -Gratitude-FINAL.pdf.

7. Iris B. Mauss et al., "Can Seeking Happiness Make People Unhappy? Paradoxical Effects of Valuing Happiness," *Emotion* 11, no. 4 (August 2011): 807–15, doi.org/10.1037/a0022010.

8. June Gruber, "Four Ways Happiness Can Hurt You," *Greater Good Magazine*, May 3, 2012, greatergood.berkeley.edu/article/item/four_ways_happiness_can_hurt_you.

9. Jennifer E. Stellar et al., "Self-Transcendent Emotions and Their Social Functions: Compassion, Gratitude, and Awe Bind Us to Others Through Prosociality," *Emotion Review* (2017): 1–8, doi.org/10.1177/1754073916684557.

CHAPTER 13: MEDITATIONS FOR SELF-LOVE AND CONFIDENCE

1. Kristin Neff, "Why Self-Compassion Trumps Self-Esteem," *Greater Good Magazine*, May 27, 2011, greatergood.berkeley.edu/article/item/try_selfcompassion.

2. Kerri Kelly, lecture, Wanderlust Wellspring Conference, Palm Springs, CA, October 27, 2018.

3. Jay R. Cambridge, phone interview, January 24, 2019.

4. Erin Falconer, phone interview, January 24, 2019.

5. Ibid.

CHAPTER 14: MEDITATIONS FOR FOCUS AND INTUITION

1. "How Porn Affects the Brain Like a Drug," Fight the New Drug (website), August 23, 2017, fightthenewdrug.org/how-porn-affects-the-brain-like-a-drug.

2. "Let's Talk about Porn. Is It as Harmless as Society Says It Is?" May 29, 2019, fightthenewdrug.org/3-reasons-why-watching-porn-is-harmful.

3. Jill Suttie, "How Nature Can Make You Kinder, Happier, and More Creative," *Greater Good Magazine*, March 2, 2016, greatergood.berkeley.edu/article/item /how_nature_makes_you_kinder_happier_more_creative.

4. Kristophe Green and Dacher Keltner, "What Happens When We Reconnect with Nature," *Greater Good Magazine*, March 1, 2017, greatergood.berkeley.edu/article/item /what_happens_when_we_reconnect_with_nature.

5. Florence Williams, *The Nature Fix* (New York: W. W. Norton, 2017).

6. Dacher Keltner et al., "The Sociocultural Appraisals, Values, and Emotions (SAVE) Framework of Prosociality: Core Processes from Gene to Meme," *Annual Review of Psychology* 65 (2014): 425–60, doi.org/10.1146/annurev-psych-010213-115054.

CHAPTER 15: MEDITATIONS FOR SOCIAL JUSTICE

1. Ethan Nichtern (@ethannichtern), Twitter, October 4, 2018, 3:03 p.m., twitter.com/i/web/status/1047955339872817152.

2. Justin Michael Williams, "Alicia Garza: The TRUTH about #BlackLivesMatter," *Motivation for Black People*, podcast interview, January 28, 2018, podcasts.apple.com/us/podcast/alicia-garza-the-truth-about-blacklivesmatter/id1341565149?i=1000400939016.

3. Justin Michael Williams, "Darnell L. Moore: Break the System Through Inner Transformation," *Motivation for Black People*, podcast interview, February 3, 2008, podcasts.apple.com/us/podcast/darnell-moore-break-system-through-inner-transformation/id1341565149?i=1000401407255.

4. Ibid.

5. "#WeVoteNext Summit: Activist Janaya 'Future' Khan on Redefining Privilege," Now This (website), video, October 28, 2018, nowthisnews.com/videos/politics/activist-janaya-future-khan-on-redefining-privilege.

6. Buzzfeed, "What Is Privilege," YouTube, video, July 4, 2015, youtube.com/watch?v=hD5f8GuNuGQ.

7. Jill Suttie, "Can Mindfulness Help Reduce Racism?" *Greater Good Magazine*, December 9, 2014, greatergood.berkeley.edu/article/item/can_mindfulness_help_reduce_racism.

8. "#WeVoteNext Summit," Now This (website).

about the author

JUSTIN MICHAEL WILLIAMS is an author and inspirational entertainer who is using music and meditation to *wake up the world*.

When he was younger, Justin always wanted to be a singer, but a lifetime of being bullied, teased, and abused made him give up his dream. Then, after a seminal moment with his dying grandmother, Justin woke up—and his debut album premiered in the top 20 of the iTunes charts next to Britney Spears and Taylor Swift. He has since been featured by Billboard, Grammy.com, SXSW, and shared stages alongside some of the most compelling leaders of our time, including Marianne Williamson, Deepak Chopra, and Chaka Khan.

With more than a decade of teaching experience, Justin has become a pioneering voice of color for the new healing movement. Between his podcast, keynotes, and motivational online platforms, Justin's teachings have now spread to more than 40 countries around the globe.

Justin is dedicated to using his voice *to serve*. To being a beacon of hope for those who are lost, and to making sure *all* people, of *all* backgrounds, have access to the information they need to change their lives.

"What inspires me most is watching people overcome incredible struggles to accomplish the things they once thought were impossible," says Williams. "When people wake up to their own brilliance—it's like magic. If my work and art can inspire people to do that, then I've fulfilled my mission."

Website: justinmichaelwilliams.com

Social media: @wejustwill

about the illustrator

VICTORIA CASSINOVA is a Los Angeles—based visual artist. Her work is rooted in the desire to inspire, to empower, and to create an experience using the art of visual communication. Through various mediums, her work has also contributed to social justice movements in order to spark inspiration and action. For more, visit vcassinova.com.

about sounds true

SOUNDS TRUE is a multimedia publisher whose mission is to inspire and support personal transformation and spiritual awakening. Founded in 1985 and located in Boulder, Colorado, we work with many of the leading spiritual teachers, thinkers, healers, and visionary artists of our time. We strive with every title to preserve the essential "living wisdom" of the author or artist. It is our goal to create products that not only provide information to a reader or listener but also embody the quality of a wisdom transmission.

For those seeking genuine transformation, Sounds True is your trusted partner. At SoundsTrue.com you will find a wealth of free resources to support your journey, including exclusive weekly audio interviews, free downloads, interactive learning tools, and other special savings on all our titles.

To learn more, please visit SoundsTrue.com/freegifts or call us toll-free at 800.333.9185.

sounds true
WAKING UP THE WORLD